PRAISE FOR *Forgiving Our...*

"I have never seen anyone truly thrive who had not forgiven their parents, even for awful things. This is a call to very hard, but very vital, work of the soul."

—DR. HENRY CLOUD
LEADERSHIP EXPERT, PSYCHOLOGIST,
AND BEST-SELLING AUTHOR

"At Focus on the Family we hear from many adults who are burdened by pain, bitterness, and deep emotional wounds as a result of parental abuse, neglect, or abandonment during childhood. I understand that pain because that was my own experience. *Forgiving Our Fathers and Mothers* is essential reading for anyone who wants to deal with those hurts in a constructive, healing, and God-honoring manner."

—JIM DALY
PRESIDENT, FOCUS ON THE FAMILY

"*Forgiving Our Mothers and Fathers* is a book of courage—the courage to listen to the Bible and the stories of others who have experienced soul-wrenching forgiveness and reconciliation, the courage to confront pain and bewilderment, the courage to enter into forgiveness in a way that both wounds and heals. Leslie Leyland Fields and Jill Hubbard take us into raw, messy stories so we can be transformed by that mysterious and painful grace in the force called forgiveness."

—SCOT MCKNIGHT
NORTHERN SEMINARY

"I loved Jill's award-winning book *The Secrets Young Women Keep*. Now *Forgiving Our Fathers and Mothers* is even better! Leslie's purposeful journey, together with Jill's experienced insights, profoundly guides us in how to live a higher calling. If you question whether or not unresolved issues with your parents are affecting your life, this is the book for you."

—STEPHEN ARTERBURN
FOUNDER AND CHAIRMAN OF NEW LIFE MINISTRIES;
HOST OF CHRISTIAN RADIO TALK SHOW *NEW
LIFE LIVE!* AND BEST-SELLING AUTHOR

"In *Forgiving Our Fathers and Mothers*, Leslie Leyland Fields and Jill Hubbard provide a gutsy, honest portrayal of the journey to honor a parent in the face of a painful legacy of neglect and abuse. Full of compassion and conviction, this book echoes the promise that one can find mercy to forgive and freedom to live, even out from under the most destructive parenting relationship. A testimony to the power of faith and the possibility of redemption, *Forgiving Our Fathers and Mothers* offers bright hope that our most defining relationships can change through the love and mercy of God that enables us to forgive."

—JAMES L. FURROW, PHD
EVELYN AND FRANK FREED PROFESSOR OF MARITAL AND
FAMILY THERAPY; CHAIR, DEPARTMENT OF MARRIAGE
AND FAMILY, FULLER THEOLOGICAL SEMINARY

"Leslie Leyland Fields's story of forgiveness of her father, and the journey that takes her on, is nothing short of amazing and inspiring! Combined with Dr. Jill Hubbard's clinical look and review at the conclusion of each chapter, this is a book for everyone. Whether it's a parent, other family member, friend, work associate, church member or neighbor, we all have forgiveness issues to deal with, and this book helps you see why and how to walk through them. It's a keeper!"

—LARRY SONNENBURG
PRESIDENT, NEW LIFE MINISTRIES

"What do we do with a mother or father who destroys a part of our soul? In *Forgiving Our Fathers and Mothers*, Leslie Leyland Fields and Jill Hubbard offer us an extraordinarily compassionate, eminently practical, and solidly Christian answer. I highly recommend this book for anyone who craves the psychological healing and spiritual renewal that can only come through forgiveness."

—PAULA HUSTON
AUTHOR OF *FORGIVENESS, THE HOLY WAY,*
AND *SIMPLIFYING THE SOUL*

"One of the most important development stages that allows us to become fully adult is to emotionally separate ourselves from our parents. To not face the reality of our childhoods and forgive our parents is to remain in emotional bondage, to limit the potential of our adult destiny that God has in store for us, and to remain perpetually defined and shaped by our families of origin.

"Leslie Leyland Fields and Dr. Jill Hubbard have teamed up to write a compelling book that helps us understand the positive impact of facing our reality, then forgiving those who have hurt us. If you want to experience more emotional freedom and feel more like an adult, then start reading this this wonderfully written book."

—MILAN & KAY YERKOVICH
COUNSELORS; AUTHORS OF *HOW WE LOVE*
AND *HOW WE LOVE OUR KIDS*

"This book is a great two-for-one! You read through Leslie's remarkable story of forgiveness and then you are challenged by Dr. Hubbard's insights and questions to bring the story home personally to each of us. You're holding a great resource on the core issue of our faith—forgiveness!"

—DAVID STOOP, PHD
AUTHOR, *FORGIVING THE UNFORGIVABLE*

Forgiving Our
FATHERS
AND
MOTHERS

Forgiving Our

FATHERS
AND
MOTHERS

Finding Freedom from Hurt and Hate

LESLIE LEYLAND FIELDS
AND DR. JILL HUBBARD

W PUBLISHING GROUP

AN IMPRINT OF THOMAS NELSON

Published in Nashville Tennessee, by W Publishing, an imprint of Thomas Nelson.

The authors are represented by, and this book is published in association with, the literary agency of WordServe Literary Group, Ltd., www.wordserveliterary.com.

Thomas Nelson titles may be purchased in bulk for educational, business, fund-raising, or sales promotional use. For information, please e-mail SpecialMarkets@ThomasNelson.com.

Library of Congress Cataloging-in-Publication Data

Fields, Leslie Leyland, 1957-
  Forgiving our fathers and mothers : finding freedom from hurt and hate / Leslie Leyland Fields and Dr. Jill Hubbard.
    pages cm
  Includes bibliographical references.
  ISBN 978-0-8499-6472-5 (trade paper)
  1. Forgiveness--Religious aspects--Christianity. 2. Families--Religious aspects--Christianity. I. Title.
  BV4647.F55F54 2014
  248.8'4--dc23

                          2013021568

Printed in the United States of America

14 15 16 17 18 19 RRD 6 5 4 3 2 1

For all those longing to be freed to forgive
and
for my brothers and sisters
who have been an essential part
of this forgiveness walk

CONTENTS

INTRODUCTION

In the desert
I saw a creature, naked, bestial,
Who, squatting upon the ground,
Held his heart in his hands,
And ate of it.
I said: "Is it good, friend?"
"It is bitter-bitter," he answered;
"But I like it
Because it is bitter,
And because it is my heart."
— STEPHEN CRANE[1]

I HADN'T SEEN my father for ten years. I had no photographs of him at all and just a vague memory of his face the last time I saw him.

When we pulled up to the VA housing complex in Sarasota in our rented van, Duncan saw him first.

"There he is." He tipped his head to point.

I turned my eyes slowly to follow his gaze, almost not wanting to look. A man was standing under the awning of the complex. It was him. I saw his dark skin, his head, nearly bald, distinctively square, with a barely visible neck. He was just as I remembered, but bigger, maybe forty pounds heavier than the last time. He was wearing shorts and a striped jersey, the shirt taut over his belly.

I stared at him, suddenly frozen. *What do I do?* I thought. *How do I play this scene? Loving daughter greeting long-lost father? Kind daughter bringing her children to meet their grandfather for the first time? Angry daughter wanting just a few words from her silent father?*

The van stopped. I got out slowly, carrying my youngest, and opened the side doors for the others. The rest of the kids piled out, five more, one after another, like some silly cartoon scene with an unending stream of people erupting from a tiny car. My father stood there, looking past the kids, seeming not to see them, as if they were inconsequential to his life—which they were. When the last one jumped out, suddenly I was on. I knew what to do. I put my toddler down and came and smiled, then hugged the strange man, patting him on the back with my fingers, keeping our bodies separate.

"Hi. How ah ya?" he asked in his Massachusetts accent. He smiled a little, showing his few remaining teeth, all broken.

"Good. We had a little trouble finding this place," I said with false brightness. It had taken us two days to get there.

We had flown in from Kodiak, Alaska, from the far northwest corner of the country to the far southeast corner. From squalls and stormy ocean to palm trees and traffic.

It was March 2006, our spring break. Through some impetus I don't remember now, I had decided we needed to go to Florida. We would do the usual vacation things, but mostly this was a trip to see my father. He was eighty-four, so I knew this would be my children's only chance to meet him.

I had never talked about him to my kids. They didn't know

anything about him, and they never asked. He knew nothing about them. But over my then twenty-eight years of marriage and sixteen years of parenting, I had learned from my husband and from my children what fathers might be for, so I wanted them to know who *my* father was, for themselves. Someday they would care.

I had warned the four older kids, ages nine to sixteen, that he probably would not talk to them or even ask their names or ages. They shrugged, accepted this as routine. I worried most about the two youngest, one and a half and three, who thought all grandfathers were like their grandpa back home, an old man who wanted you to sit on his knee, who played hide-and-seck with you, and who asked you questions and gave you hugs. So I didn't tell them the man in front of them was their grandfather. I just told them this man was my father. Even that felt like a deception.

We decided, finally, on a trip to the beach and loaded into the van, nine of us now, and drove to Sarasota Beach, on his suggestion. I had no idea what to do on this visit and felt saved by this beach. It was blindingly white, as deep as it was wide, bodies massed on sand and in water. I walked slowly with my father out onto the sand—he walked like the old man he now was. I did not give him my arm. Duncan and the kids ran ahead into the water while I scoped out a stamp of ground for our blanket.

Finding one, I spread the blanket and plopped down. "Can you sit?" I asked, looking up at my aged father as he stood above me.

"No, my hips are bad," he said matter-of-factly. He couldn't lower himself onto the sand. I had no idea what to do. I hadn't considered this possibility.

A man nearby heard our dilemma and jumped up to offer his own folding chair; I felt a sudden bright heat—yes, kindness. I understood as I set up the chair. Later I would get my father a hot dog, then an ice cream. I began to understand. Maybe I could pity him. Surely I could feel pity for this old man. And I could pretend that this was all of my grief, simply the diminishments of age.

We sat there in the white sun on the white beach, just he and I. This was my last chance to know who he was, to find a fissure, something to take me down into that frozen stillness. I asked him about the war, about his mother and father, about his childhood— I knew so little. He didn't remember much, answering in short, vague sentences spoken sideways, his eyes always away, looking to the ocean. I was bothering him. He wanted to sit in the sun, watch the water, and be quiet. I kept asking questions, trying to store some of his words in my head to write down later, but they evaporated almost as soon as he spoke them.

Two hours later, we were headed back, the day at the beach already exhausted. I was quiet and grim. Had we really spent all that money to fly down here for just two hours? He hadn't asked the names of my children or spoken to them, except to ask the older ones about the weather in Kodiak. Wanting something to claim from this visit, I suggested one more stop before we let him off—ice cream. We stood in line for our cones, then ate them under a tree as we watched the traffic.

Just before we left the soft-serve stand, I told Duncan to take a photo. I wanted to remember this moment, the last time I would see my father. He sat at the wooden picnic table with a slight smirk, looking utterly content. I stood behind him, deciding not to arrange my face. I would let it be. My lips taut, mouth clamped shut, containing as much emptiness and want as I could hold. And anger at myself and him. *How can I still want?* I mused. *How can I forgive him for all the years past, for this moment even now? He is utterly content with his ice cream, while his daughter sits beside him, starving to death—and the ice cream is pretty good today, isn't it?*

I would not come back, I decided. It was the same as always. He had no interest in being a father and less interest in his third daughter. I was done. I felt a kind of relief that I could finally close that door.

———

Four years later, I was reciting the Lord's Prayer. I was awake—I feel sure I was awake—when I came to these strange words: *Forgive us our sins, as we have forgiven those who sin against us* (Matt. 6:12 NLT). I stopped, eyes wide. What was *that* word doing there, that *as?* What was I asking?

How many times have I said these words and not heard this? I wondered. *I am asking God to base his forgiveness of me on my forgiveness of others? Surely that's a slip, a scribe's slide of the pen. How can God's forgiveness be dependent upon my forgiveness?* I did not want to, but I immediately thought of my father, that inanimate bulk of a human being who kept getting in the way.

There was more. I kept hearing the commandment, "Honor your father and your mother" (Ex. 20:12). And I wondered as I thought about my apathetic father, *How do I honor this man?* The question came as a deep puzzle to me, as it did to all my siblings. But I was not so cut off in my hurt that I did not know how many others were in the same dilemma. So many other daughters and sons, regardless of age: middle-aged adults, young adults, teens. *Does "Honor your father" apply to us,* I questioned, *those of us who have been hurt and deceived and abandoned by our mothers or fathers, or even both? Surely if they are dishonorable, we need not honor them! We're off the hook*. Neither did I care to forgive my father and all that had been done in the rooms and houses of my childhood where he sometimes sat and walked—and walked away from.

And suddenly, the way such things happen, all the world felt abuzz with this issue. I chanced to sit beside a friend on a plane just as I was returning from a visit with my father. She told me about her own father, who was schizophrenic and institutionalized, and who had made her life miserable. She was relieved when he died.

"How can you be so serene about all this now?" I asked.

"I've forgiven him," she said simply.

While I was in Memphis to lead a seminar, the woman who was housing and feeding me told me about her father, how he had left her family when she was in high school, without a word, to live with another woman. And after ten years of silence, he wanted back in her life. "I don't want to let him in," she shared. "I know I should forgive him, but I can't."

A friend was taking care of his elderly mother. One day he shared his feelings with me. "She's an alcoholic," he told me darkly. "It's hard. I know I need to forgive her, but I don't know how."

Another time, I talked to a counselor at a Christian college. "You wouldn't believe how many issues young people have with their parents," she said. "This is the time in their lives, when they first leave home, when they really see what they've come from. Most want to forgive their parents, but it's very hard for them."

"I left home very young," a young man told me. "I couldn't live with my mother anymore. I don't even want to forgive her."

An online friend wrote, "Can I talk to you about this— forgiving my father? I am so in trouble on this issue!"

One of my students, Allison, wrote an essay about her alcoholic mother: "I believe that lament is a common story for all of us.

Bad things happen. Mothers (and fathers) fail. But I'm wondering if I've lived in the land of lament too long, and if it's time to piece these stories together in a different way. I wonder if it's time to forgive. I have no idea how to do this."

The messages were everywhere. I could not seem to escape them or the media. Every form of it—radio, e-mails, magazines, online articles—carried messages on forgiveness, words like these: *When you cling to bitterness, you are caged in emotions you cannot control. You need to set yourself free.* A more specific message, from psychologists and mental health professionals, went like this: *You can't grow up and be full adults until you can forgive your parents. End the cycle of hurt and disappointment that stalls you and keeps your children continually needy and continually bruised by the parent who can't meet their needs.* Messages from pastors and priests said, *You are to forgive others as God has forgiven you.* TV talk shows opined, *If you really want to be happy, you need to forgive those who have hurt you. It's the true road to freedom and happiness!*

The medical profession has discovered the health benefits of forgiveness. They've found that people who were able to release their offenders from their own anger and judgment improved their health, lowering blood pressure and heart rate and decreasing their levels of depression, anxiety, and anger.[2]

In the political realm, within the last thirty years, the practice of forgiveness has been embraced by government leaders all over the world as the best hope for healing fractured peoples and nations. South Africa, Northern Ireland, Sierra Leone, and Rwanda are some of the hotbeds of bloodshed and violence where forgiveness projects are releasing ethnic and religious groups from generational cycles of revenge and retaliation, changing the culture.

In the United States, forgiveness has become a legitimate and hopeful area of academic study. In 1994 Robert D. Enright, along with the Human Development Study Group at the University of Wisconsin–Madison, founded the International Forgiveness Institute in the belief that forgiveness could help those who had experienced abuse and violence. More than this, however, Enright and his colleagues saw forgiveness as a potent force that could bring restoration and harmony between hostile parties. Enright used a twenty-step forgiveness model in Northern Ireland for mothers and relatives who had lost family members in the sectarian violence and whose lives were stuck in grief and hatred.

More recently, the Stanford Forgiveness Project, begun in 2001, researches and explores ways that forgiveness could end social and familial ruptures.

In America, we face a daunting need for forgiveness, especially within our own homes. And the need will only continue to grow. As the American family evolves, more than half of all children are born outside of marriage, leaving an increasing number of children fatherless and living below the poverty line.[3] Both of these factors increase the chances for child abuse and neglect, which are at record numbers today. And the numbers continue to climb. Authorities received more than three million calls concerning more than six million children at risk in 2012. The United States has the worst record among industrialized countries: more than five children a day die from abuse and neglect, and likely the numbers are much higher.[4] These are tragic statistics, and they remind us, in the words of Christian editor and author Rodney Clapp, that "every night we lock ourselves behind doors with the people most likely to hurt us."[5]

What does all of this have to do with forgiveness? Clearly, as a nation, within our families there is much to be forgiven. If we are to thrive as human beings, if our countries and our communities are to prosper, if our families are to flourish, we will need to learn and practice ways of forgiving those who have had the greatest impact upon us: our mothers and fathers. Most of the time this will not mean simply our birth mothers and fathers. Many of us have an array of parental figures in our lives: parents-in-law, stepparents, foster parents, adoptive parents, godparents, and those who were charged to mentor us in motherly and fatherly ways. Some excelled in these roles. Others did not. Many inflicted hurt instead.

As I first began to listen and take notes, forgiveness sounded so necessary and so alluring. (Freedom? Happiness? Better health? No longer under my offenders' emotional control?) But because I'm slow and stubborn, and because my life is so busy, only gradually did I begin to reach this simple conviction: I must forgive my father. There were others, too, whom I knew I needed to forgive. They suddenly sprang full-bodied before me as I wrote—a man no longer living, a former pastor, a long-ago friend—but my attention was first seized by my father.

I knew at the same time that forgiveness was a necessary passage for all sons and daughters. And that my own path, though at times it would feel lonely, would not be singular or solitary. Many were walking along with me, lots of them ahead of me, some behind, some hesitating and balking at the start line as I did for so many years, but most of us believing we *should* forgive our fathers and mothers. And in moments of stronger conviction: we *must* forgive our fathers and mothers.

I know even now as I write these words that challenges will come. For those who have suffered at the hands of the very ones who were to cherish and nurture them, the first question is, *why* should I forgive? It's one of the best questions I know. I have asked it myself, sometimes in anger, other times in sincere disbelief. Often after hearing stories like the ones in these pages, we are compelled to ask, "*Why* pluck these mothers and fathers off the hook of their own guilt? *Why* let them go free from the judgment and consequences they deserve? Is that what forgiveness means?" There are answers to this, I have found—profound answers that shake the very ground we stand on, answers that will likely affect all other relationships around us as well.

These aren't the only questions. We also ask:

"How do I honor parents who are dishonorable?"

"Can I still forgive my parents even though they're no
longer living?"

"I don't want to be reconciled to my mother. Does
forgiveness require reconciliation?"

"If I am supposed to forgive, then *how* do I forgive?"

This book will address all these questions, not by simple proclamation, but through show-and-tell. I will provide the "show" through my own story and through the lives of others—people like Vonnie, Gayle, Jimmy, William, and many more, real people who are wrestling with the same questions you are. I will follow their stories and my own with as much honesty as we can allow.

Dr. Jill Hubbard, a clinical psychologist, Gold Medallion–nominated author, and radio and television personality who has practiced in the mental health field for more than twenty-five years, will provide the "tell," concluding each chapter with clear application and study questions to guide you in your own walk. Her passion for joining me in this project is rooted in her belief in the therapeutic healing benefits and necessity of an intentional process of forgiveness. She has walked countless clients down this path and has embraced it as her own life-stance for navigating through difficult and very personal forgiveness issues.

Between the two of us, we are writers, editors, researchers, teachers, counselors, and mothers. We will include our considerable research and interviews, but what qualifies us most for this work is that we are both daughters—daughters who have been immersed in our own work of parental forgiveness.

A question comes to me even as I am writing this: Do we really need another book on forgiveness? My need to write it—and the fact that you're reading these pages now—tells the answer. The topic does not go away, because we keep on hurting one another, failing our most essential relationships, and being plagued—even haunted—by the events in our past. But it does not go away for a deeper reason, I suspect. I am wondering at the quality of our forgiveness of one another, and specifically of our fathers and mothers, the purview of this book. I can speak to the quality of my own—how temporary and superficial it often is, dependent on emotions and circumstances. I think of how selfish my motives have been—to forgive my father for my own sake. I know this is important. I know we must do it for ourselves, but as I began to consider forgiveness more deeply, I became troubled by the messages I was hearing from the general media and the religious media alike. Even in something this divine and holy—because we must admit: forgiveness is, in many ways, against our natural human inclinations—even here, we hold fast to our self-focus and are enticed to forgive for *our* sakes, because it frees *us*. We are counseled to work at a small, private forgiveness, not for something much larger than us that reaches from our individual lives out into the larger world. This book will begin at the point of our greatest pain and will move us, chapter by chapter, beyond, into a place of freedom that we cannot even imagine now, a freedom that promises to begin to heal the brokenness of the world itself.

To get there, we'll be following stories that are far from simple. They will be as complicated as the people telling them and living them. But lest you open this book ready to flinch at horrific stories of abuse and despair, let me reassure you. This book will be neither a catalog of dysfunction and despair nor a competition for the most vile transgressions visited upon a child. The news already contains too many of these realities. Yes, there will be some hard stories here—and there will be some easy stories. Not all is life-and-death, hurt and despair. Sometimes what catches in our throats is a word, a gesture, a meal of mackerel we couldn't face every week for a year, the buckled galoshes and boy clothes we girls had to wear to school. (Ah yes, Laurie and Jan, remember the boy galoshes and how we were endlessly teased about them?) The ordinary injustices that grow from a rub into an irritant, something we can't quite shake. Sharon's mother fed her frozen mixed vegetables nearly every night, she thinks. "To this day I can't eat them," she told me, laughing. "You know: those little cubed carrots?" But my hope is that among these stories of the everyday and the exceptional, you will find a way to move forward in your own necessary journey.

There are many reasons to begin this path: To silence your memories. To forget what's been done to you. To unlock your own hard heart and walk about free. To do good to someone who doesn't deserve it. To restore a relationship. Whatever your motives, you are the one to do it. You cannot wait for your father and mother to do this for you. You cannot wait for them any longer.

ONE

Becoming Jonah: Running from Our Stories

*Oh yes, the past can hurt. But the way I see it, you can either run
from it, or learn from it.*

—Rafiki, from *The Lion King*[1]

It's my wedding day. We've just finished our last finals for the
fall semester. Now, two days later, Duncan and I are getting
married.

I am not a princess bride; I am wearing a wedding dress bor-
rowed from my English professor. The dress is fifteen years out of
date, and it doesn't fit me very well. I know I don't look beautiful in
it, but it cost nothing, and I am honored that my English prof, whom
I admire, has offered it to me. I will do my own makeup and hair.

The church was decorated by my friends, who hung fresh pine
boughs cut from nearby trees. Our budget for the wedding is three
hundred dollars. I have no idea who is supposed to pay for and do
what. (I've been to a single wedding in my life.) But at the age of
just-turned twenty, it is scandalous to me to think of parents being
involved in our wedding. Luckily, neither mother cares. Duncan's

parents and younger brother have flown down from Alaska to this small church in Ohio, that Duncan and I attend. His grandmother is here from Oklahoma. His older brother and sister-in-law are here from Indiana.

On my side of the church sit my mother and youngest brother, who drove down from New Hampshire two days before the wedding. My father is working in a shoe factory—throwing hides onto a stamping machine—the first regular job he's had. He will not come. My other two brothers are working and cannot get time off; my two sisters have small children and have no way to get here. But even having two here is something. I'm grateful for their presence.

The wedding march plays. The small church is full, mostly of congregants who have so generously embraced us. I am partly afraid. What am I doing? I feel as though I am the maker of my own future, which thrills me but scares me as well.

I am walking alone down the aisle—of course! Wasn't I the one who made it here, to this altar, by herself? At twenty, I have been running my own life for a while, and I don't need my first walk with my father to begin now, down this wedding aisle. The lace carpet is the runway to my future. Duncan and I will live in Alaska, on a small wilderness island. We will commercial fish. We will travel. We will build a new life together, five thousand miles away from the claustrophobic houses and small towns I grew up in. Surely that is far enough away to be freed from the past and to become the person I want to be.

———

My sister Laurie ran away from home at fifteen. I did not know the details until the writing of this book. She ran away at night many times, opening the window, stooping to get through, dropping to the ground, and running two miles in the night to her friend's house, a shack on a backwoods dirt road. She would vow each time that she'd never go back home, but the next morning she would walk back before my mother's wake-up call for school.

But one night the pattern ended. She gathered some essentials in a bag and left near midnight. He was there to pick her up, her then seventeen-year-old boyfriend, with his hopped-up car. His family had an old trailer in the woods that no one else knew about. They went there, Laurie now feeling a mix of sickness and freedom. What would happen when everyone got up at 6:30 a.m. and she wasn't there? Right then she didn't care.

When we saw the next morning that she was gone, we weren't surprised. Laurie was different from the rest of us. She was dark and moody, withdrawn. We lived in rural New Hampshire, and the rest of us escaped the house when our work was finished as often as we could and spent long days in the woods, on the skating pond, on the hill behind our house, in the field across the street. We had few neighbors. Friends couldn't come over. We were one another's friends and playmates—but Laurie often would not join us. She hung back and did . . . I don't know what she did, but it seemed she wasn't around very much, and when she was, there was some kind of trouble. She played with her kneecaps incessantly one year, until she pushed it too far and couldn't walk. She fell down the stairs one night when the six of us were alone at home. She was twelve, I think, and lying there, hurt. We didn't know what to do. But we knew if it were to happen to anyone, it would be Laurie. She was a dark presence among us.

We didn't know where she was for months, though the police were looking for her. We didn't know why she left, just that she was always unhappy. I wished her well but was not concerned for her. I didn't know enough about the world to be concerned. I just knew she was freed from our house—and I was glad for her. (Now, looking back, I can imagine much better how difficult it was for my mother.)

The trailer was finally found one day, months later, but Laurie refused to return. Three years later, when she turned eighteen, she came back to marry her boyfriend before a justice of the peace.

There are so many ways to run.

William grew up with a volatile, hostile mother. He left home for college, then married and returned only for rare visits.

Vonnie ran from her house into the arms of a boyfriend, marrying him at nineteen.

Randi tried disappearing through anorexia and excessive workouts, running out her rage on the road and track every day.

Dena immersed herself in her children and her new life, pretending everything was fine.

Lisa refused communication with her father, who abandoned her family while she was in high school.

Jimmy became engrossed in achievement, deciding he would be the best at whatever he turned his hand to.

We go off to college, to early marriages, to early parenthood, to jobs. We grow up and leave our parents' houses, often too soon, sometimes not soon enough. We don't always know we are running from what's behind us—sometimes we are so numbed to our pasts that we think only of running into our futures. Almost always there is silence as we each desperately work at building a new life, a new identity. This is the second runaway: we will not listen or attend to what we've left behind. We leave through the doors, and we think the new houses we choose are distant and safe. But the construct seldom holds.

Dena kept having panic attacks while shopping or cleaning the house, ordinary things in a life she thought was fixed and "normal."

Vonnie's marriage collapsed into an acrid divorce, plunging her into alcoholism, a series of boyfriends, and a brush with suicide.

Lisa brought her suppressed past into her marriage, viewing her husband with suspicion. Her father had been an adulterer and had abandoned her. Her husband would as well, she knew.

Nudges and prods, tentacles from our earlier lives, reach in. Meanwhile, Mother's Day and Father's Day pop up on the calendar every year. Don't we all know what it's like to read every single card on the rack—all those verses about love and gratitude, how our parents were always there for us and how much they listened, how thoughtful they've been all through the years—and then to put each one back, reaching instead for the blank card, where we could write about the weather? Maybe someone will create a line of cards that better fit our lives: "Thanks, Dad, for, uh, doing your part in siring me." "Thanks so much, Mom, for giving me . . . well, for giving me life." "Happy Father's Day, Dad. Thanks for not yelling at me as much as you could have."

Or maybe we go to a movie or a play, and there's a moment of such tenderness between a father or mother and a child that we suck in our breath. Maybe we cry. I went to a seminar one year called The Blessing, about parents handing down a legacy, giving their children their blessing and support as they move out into life. How many have received this? I ran out of the auditorium, sobbing. Why didn't we all run out?

These reminders are not always painful. After speaking at a Christian college at homecoming, I was led into the inner sanctum, the cherry-paneled dining room saved for the speakers and the potential donors. I sat down awkwardly for lunch with the president and assorted faculty. Halfway through the meal, the president turned to me and asked, "What does your father do?"

I looked at him, puzzled. I was thirty-six at the time, with a husband and three children. I had left home nineteen years ago. My parents had divorced ten years earlier. I had no contact with my father. So what did I say to the immaculate, designer-suited college president over our linen napkins and exquisite food? My mind whirled while I decided how to answer. But it suddenly hit me—I knew what he was asking. I told the bald truth.

"He was a traveling salesman, but he couldn't sell anything, so he was unemployed a lot. He works in a factory now. He's an atheist."

The president blinked, eyes widened for a half second, and his smile went plastic while he nodded, and then he turned away. He barely spoke to me the rest of the lunch. I'm out, then. I am judged and found wanting—because of my father.

No matter how fleet your feet, how far you travel, those days come. Phone calls come in the afternoon, in the middle of your life, and everything changes. Vonnie's sister called her one day. "Mom's dying. She wants to see you." Vonnie was dropping her kids off at school. How could she go see her mother? It had been twenty years since she had seen her—and still the fear was there. She should go, she knew. It was the right thing to do—but how?

Vonnie, shaking with the return of suppressed memories, drove to her doctor's office and walked up to the window. The receptionist looked up at her, their eyes met, and Vonnie burst into tears. When the doctor heard her story, he set up an appointment with a counselor.

Over the next few days with the counselor, Vonnie recognized that she still loved her mother, as hard as it was to admit it. She realized maybe she had loved her all along, but her mother could never love her back. "It was okay for me to say I loved her, but she couldn't love me," she said. "When I realized the truth of that, it was a weight off my shoulders. I felt like finally I had some control." Shortly after those emergency visits with the counselor, Vonnie decided she would go see her mother.

Her hands shook as she entered the driveway; she was still fearful. Moments later, she entered the bedroom and looked cautiously at the woman in the bed—white-haired, her eyes shut. She was frail, crippled, unable to talk or move or feed herself—the final days of Alzheimer's, her sister told her. She hadn't recognized anyone in a while.

Vonnie sat beside her on the bed. The dying mother opened her eyes, not focused, and started to move them around. She saw Vonnie, her oldest child, and whispered to her, "I shouldn't have been so hard on you." Then Vonnie's mother cried. It was the first time Vonnie had turned around to look behind her. And it began to change her life.

A phone call from a sister broke into my life as well. It was two or three years after my family's visit to Sarasota. The call came while I was fixing supper and coaching homework, settling disputes between brothers, working on a book in my head—all the things my life was overflowing with.

"Dad fell down on the sidewalk walking back from the store last week. He couldn't get up. An ambulance came—he's out of the hospital now. They thought he might have had a little heart attack. I just found out today."

My father was in his mid-eighties by then. How surprising could this news be, especially since he'd smoked all his life, and his favorite food was ice cream? The larger question was, why had he lived *this* long? But I instantly saw him, fallen on the sidewalk, helpless, with a few people gathering, and felt a piercing stab in my gut. *That's my father.* And I knew that had he died, we would not have heard about it for . . . how long? Maybe a week. He had not told anyone in his housing complex that he had children.

"How did you find out, Laurie?"

"I talked to Dad on the phone today."

Silence. Then, "You're talking to Dad?"

"Yes. I've been calling him almost every week," she said, her voice calm and assured.

"Does he talk to you? What do you talk about?" I could not hide my amazement and confusion. I couldn't believe that out of the six of us, she was the one calling him.

"Yeah, he talks. I ask him about things. He'll answer. Sometimes I'm on the phone with him for forty-five minutes."

I didn't quite believe this. "But what does he say? He's never talked to us before."

"I don't know. We just talk about whatever's going on."

I was silent for a moment, then asked, "Why are you doing this, Laurie?"

"I just think he needs someone to care about him." She said it simply, without judgment.

That was a new thought. I wasn't sure about it. Why Laurie? Dad was the very reason she had run away from home.

The children, the victims, are not the only ones who flee. My father ran away too. When he was employed, he was a traveling salesman and dressed in a suit every morning, drank instant coffee, and left the house. He'd drive all day, sometimes all week, around New England, paying for his own gas and own time, stopping to drink coffee in small cafés and Friendly's ice cream shops, an unheard-of luxury in our family's nonexistent economy. He dreamed of a final good-bye, sailing alone around the world for the rest of his life.

When my mother and father divorced, finally, when we were all out of the house, he fled to Florida and stayed there, living on a twenty-eight-foot, derelict sailboat, thousands of miles from his family. He came back home just once, for two nights, for a family reunion, but only because my brother drove two thousand miles down to Florida to get him, then drove him all the way back to Florida the next day.

We've all run, fugitives from our own stories, our pasts. But sometimes we are running from a future as well, a future we cannot imagine, one we don't want a part in creating. I know of someone who did this. You may know him too. He was living whatever a normal life looked like twenty-eight hundred years ago, a man with a job to keep, bills to pay, parents to please. And then—"the word of the LORD came to" him, and we know it's going to mean trouble.[2]

It did, indeed. The world was a mess, of course, but it was a manageable mess, it seemed to Jonah. His own life was hardly a party, but it was *his* life, and he knew where to go when things got hard. He had his buddies; he had his haunts and hangouts. He knew where to worship, too, because he was not just a regular guy. He was a prophet, and he had work to do, words of God to speak. But now he was being asked to step outside of the life he knew and managed.

"Go to the great city of Nineveh and preach against it, because its wickedness has come up before me," God said (Jonah 1:2). God rang his bell, which He has every right to do.

We know what comes next. We've all heard this story since childhood; even those of us who weren't raised in Sunday school may have somehow heard this fantastical tale of a man who ran away from God and got swallowed by a whale, and three days later got vomited out. (Did I spoil the ending for anyone? So sorry!) That's what kids remember—Jonah, the upchucked prophet. But for us here and now, Jonah's story echoes into our own. He'd been called to a great, wicked city located in a neighboring country. They were enemies with Jonah and his countrymen, by reason of birth and by reason of their own violence and cruelty. They'd done his people wrong, maybe even done Jonah himself wrong. He had reason to hate them. And now he had to go and preach to them.

Preaching against them wasn't the problem. The problem was, he was ordered to warn them of their coming fate—they'd be destroyed if they didn't repent.

Destruction? Total destruction? Why should they be warned? Jonah must have thought. *Why give the chance to repent?* How many times had Israel herself been destroyed, and judgment not been withheld? Oh, the bitter taste of this, to be forced to preach "Repent!" to enemies deserving only of death! To be compelled to offer mercy to those who had not been merciful! What kind of God was this, who did not honor boundaries and simple, decent justice?

He could not bear it. So he ran. He's one of us. Yes, to the ship bound the other way. And don't we do this? We never run toward what must be done. Instead, we run precisely the other way. It's logical; it makes complete sense—until we remember God. Until we remember who He is and that this is His world, not ours. And we realize the absurdity of trying to outrun the only One.

Yet we do it again and again. This book almost didn't happen. After believing I was called to write it (no, not a voice from heaven, but almost), I ran from it. I ignored it for almost two years, busying myself with everything else. To turn around and marinate for two years in a life and memories I've spent my energies escaping—why would I do that? Why would any of us make that turn back?

But I know why. I met Vonnie while speaking at a seminar. She came up to me after the last session, a woman about my age with a clear, open face and long hair. She came to greet me with a friend, who was clearly there to support her. What would she ask or tell me that she needed such support?

"My son. He just wrote me and told me he's become an atheist. I don't know exactly why, but I realized I hadn't told him my story."

I smiled encouragingly to her, understanding how we hide things from our children.

"He doesn't know what happened to me and how God rescued me. I realized I need to write my story down. Do you have any suggestions on how I can do that?"

Oh, good, I thought. *This is easy.* I knew just the book to recommend. I named the book, and she wrote it down.

Her friend nudged her shoulder. "Tell her. Tell her about it."

I was tired—I'd spoken multiple times in the last two days, but there was something compelling about this woman. I motioned to the chairs behind us and moved to sit down. "I would love to hear."

She began, and I listened, appalled, as her story unwound. I didn't want to believe what she was telling me. I didn't want to believe what her parents had done to her. I wanted to think she was disturbed, one of those people who conjure up fantastic stories of abuse, a victim junkie who cannot form an identity or sense of worth without the pity and attention of others. But as she spoke, I knew her words were true. I saw it on her face and on her friend's face.

When she was done, I let silence settle around us for a moment. Then I said, "You're right. *You must* write down your story, Vonnie. Not just for your son. But for yourself. It is your heritage, as ugly and horrific as it is." I paraphrased one of my favorite quotes from Patricia Hampl, a reminder that we are entrusted with our pasts, and we must make something out of "the burden of our witnessing."[3]

She nodded. She knew, and now I know too. I have believed in this all my life, the power of language to bring us to truth and to freedom. Don't we all believe that "the truth will set us free"?[4] I have spent much of my professional life teaching others to do this, and I have done it myself. I spent eight years writing a difficult memoir of my own life, past and present. Like other memoir instructors, I tell my students to face their dragons, their witches in the well, and to enter the dark woods.

I tell them this because I want them to write about things that matter rather than things that are trivial and merely entertaining. But there are deeper reasons as well. When we run from our stories, we are running from our very selves, and we run great risks. Our memories form the very underpinning of our identities, even "the texture of our souls," as Dr. Dan Allender and Don Hudson wrote. "Forgetting is a wager we all make on a daily basis and it exacts a terrible price. The price of forgetting is a life of repetition, an insincere way of relating, a loss of self." This is a large enough price—to not know who we are. But the true cost is even greater than this. In the same essay Allender rightly suggests that every hurt and disaster is also a chance for redemption. When we ignore and try to suppress the past, "we lose another moment to experience God's mysterious redemption in our lives."[5]

Is it naive to think redemption is possible, even in the hardest stories? Is this fairy-tale wish fulfillment, believing that every "once upon a time" finishes with "happily every after"? Even in my own small story, I have had large doubts—uncertainties that have kept me safely distant.

There are such logical reasons to run—and to doubt. We're running from our stories, from the pages written behind us, and from an outcome we can't foresee and may not really want. Can our parents really change? Can we? How can love be wrung from a stone—or even harder, how can forgiveness be wrung from a stone and handed to someone who does not deserve it?

Now you hold this book in your hand. Maybe the running stops here, and there is enough courage to move forward out of your old story and into a new one. Like Jonah. He ran, and then the story gets better—which is to say, worse. The wailing wind and storm on the sea, the plunging ship, the white waves on the pitching deck, until Jonah was found, the fugitive.

He had been cowering in the hold for hours, waiting for God to notice his invisibility. But when the crew found him, he gained courage to finally act. People would die if he did not act and act rightly immediately!

He did. He confessed. It was his fault. He was running away from God. And he urged the sailors to throw him into the sea, so that they all might be saved. Yes, he might die, but if they didn't give him over to the wrath of God, they would all die.

We stop somewhere. Picking up this book might be the first step for some, the first time to slow down long enough to consider—maybe it's time. No one can run forever.

I stopped too. Here I am. So began the return of my father to my life. Or rather, my return to his life. And the real travel I had put off for so long—the walk down the road of forgiveness—began. I did not want this particular expedition in my life. I am busy. I'm a writer, an editor, a speaker, a mother of six. I work in commercial fishing. I had no room or time for a man who had caused nothing but harm in my life. But I know now that had I not listened and attended to this pull toward obedience, I would have missed the most staggering displays of God's character and heart.

This is waiting for you as well.

AFTERWORD . . . WITH DR. JILL

Our fathers and mothers have the wonderful opportunity of being our first relationships, setting the stage for all other relating. Our parents conceive us, carry us, give birth to us, and bring us home to an environment that is the incubator from which we emerge as the people we become.

In an ideal, Norman Rockwell world, we'd find the nurture, encouragement, and healthy modeling that would shape an exciting journey to maturity. Sadly, the stories we've just heard smack of something much different. These were not stories of loving, adoring moms and dads who gave just the right amount of care and attention. These were not parents who movingly mirrored back our uniquely individual endearing qualities and enduring characteristics.

The reflection that comes back from these parental mirrors seems murky at best, offering neglect, distance, lack of connection, and emotional blindness. Perhaps these fathers and mothers would give a nod to wanting and loving their children but are deeply mired in their own unprocessed, unresolved pasts. They simply are not adequately emotionally available for, or capable of, parenthood.

What does a child make of a reflection that doesn't match his own experience? If this scenario occurs repeatedly, and to the degree that it becomes the norm, the child begins to constantly doubt himself or feel confused. Often a parent's own history of abuse, harshness, problems, and disappointments overflow to the children. Unfortunately, many of us repeat even the most harmful of behaviors modeled by our parents—unless we recognize and confront them.

Leslie had a father who wouldn't connect, no matter how hard she tried. There was no fantasy she could conjure up to deflect the hard truth of the emptiness she experienced with him. Thankfully, Vonnie, with the encouragement of a caring friend by her side, reached out to Leslie, who was willing to be available and listen. Three women sat together and invested the love and energy to truly *connect, hear,* and *know.* Vonnie and her friend, with Leslie, helped each other to not be alone, to bear the unbearable, and to take one more step forward on the path to healing and forgiveness. To be completely known by others and still completely loved fosters deep and lasting healing.

Consider the model of Jesus Christ. In the story of the Samaritan woman at the well, a Jewish man, Jesus, to the shock of His own traveling companions, dared to engage this woman, seen as beneath Him in that day and time, in conversation. After they spoke, "the woman left her water jar beside the well and ran back to the village, telling everyone, 'Come and see a man who told me everything I ever did!'" (John 4:28–29 NLT). This woman had spent her life running and hiding in illicit relationships. When what is reflected back to us rings true and fits with who we are, we feel known and seen. Jesus gave this woman respect as a person, apart from her behavior. As He lovingly revealed her life, she felt safe enough to tell the truth. She was able to receive the joy and healing of being out of hiding and in the light. She was free to run toward others, toward fruitful connection.

A parent's impact is indescribably huge. Even in the face of facts, a child will often believe, *My parent is right, because after all, he (or she) is my parent, and he is big and I am small, so I must be wrong.* Children then change their perceptions to match what they hear and see. When a parent cannot accurately mirror and contain a child's thoughts and feelings, what gets reflected back to the child is that he or she is all alone. Kids may tell themselves things like, *I'm too much for my mom* or *I'm not enough to hold my dad's interest.*

Developmentally, children are egocentric. They see others' actions or reactions as a result of, or in relation to, themselves. Think of it like this: if I need you for my primary care and sustenance, then you are central to my life, and therefore, we revolve around each other.

It's only gradually, as children grow, that they learn separateness of body, space, ideas, and influence. I often remind my clients that at any given time we can tap into any age we've been; when hurt is triggered, we often react from a much younger emotional place than our chronological ages. When we connect the dots of past events with our present triggers and then bring them into safe relationship, we begin to integrate the sequestered, broken parts of our lives.

When we don't make the connections, we run.

Study Questions

1. Do you ever feel like Jonah, as though you're running away from something you're supposed to do? Have you experienced this in relation to anyone in your family?

2. Are you aware of the ways in which your running plays out (avoidance, busyness, alcohol, overeating, etc.), especially when the situation involves certain family members? And like Jonah, are you consumed by feelings (anger, anxiety, fear, depression) that you can't run far enough from?

3. How well are your forms of running working for you? What would happen if you didn't run? Give an example of how running away

from the pain of your past may be keeping you from fulfilling your calling or purpose in life.

4. What does your "belly of a whale" look like? What excuses or beliefs swallow you up and keep you from facing your truth and pain?

5. As you read this chapter, what specific situations in your life came to mind?

6. Read John 4:1–30, about the woman at the well. Is there anyone in your life who knows your whole story? Or a part of it? If so, who? Is that person still in your life? If not, why not?

7. What were the circumstances in which you told this person your story?

8. What factors help you in determining your ability and willingness to be vulnerable with another person?

9. Did those with whom you shared your story respond in a similar way or differently than those who hurt you? Was this experience affirming or another reoccurring event?

10. What feelings and thoughts were you left with after you shared your story? Were you able to completely disclose it? Why or why not?

———————————————————————

TWO

Daring to Confess:
The Sins of the Fathers

Why must holy places be dark places?
> —C. S. Lewis[1]

Forgive me, Father, for my father has sinned.
> —Leslie Leyland Fields

MY FATHER WAS eighty-eight, and he'd had to leave the Jefferson Center, where he'd lived for thirteen years, the month before. He couldn't pass inspection. I was not surprised. Four years earlier, when I visited with my kids, he had walked us from the lobby to the elevator, then down the hallway to his room. He'd unlocked the door slowly, opened it. "I cleaned up for you," he had said, grimacing as he waved around the room, showing us the results: a narrow box of a room, awash in old newspapers, stacks of magazines, and ashtrays. A bed and a couch took up most of the floor space. Everything was dirty. There was so little to see; he had shown me his refrigerator and the contents of his freezer—mostly cheap TV dinners and ice cream. My brother told me he had eaten ice cream before bed every night of his life since the divorce. Coffee in the morning, cigarettes all day, ice cream at night. That was all he needed. Somehow he had managed to pass his inspections for four more years. I don't know how. But now—a nursing home. A much smaller room. The beginning of the long slide.

Laurie told me all this in a phone call. We were talking more now, talking about him. When did it happen, that crack in the plaster of my heart? Perhaps it was something said in a phone call. A passage I read in the book of Micah one morning, a stunning sentence that I could pitch my whole life upon: "He has showed you, O man, what is good. . . . To act justly and to love mercy and to walk humbly with your God" (6:8). Yes, I prayed. Let me "act justly," whatever that might mean. Let me "love mercy," though I was not sure I wanted to. But kindness? Yes. Kindness, like the man offering a chair to my father on the beach. I could do that. And let me humble myself before God and go to see him.

But what would come of it? Would this trip be any different from the last one, a trip that ended in bitterness? And the one before that?

I thought of that trip, fourteen years before. In the previous ten years I had seen him only once. He was living on a sailboat then, moored in Captain Jack's marina in Sarasota. His lifelong dream had been to sail around the world. Books and magazines with sailboats floated on our tables and bookshelves for most of my childhood.

I remember arriving and meeting him at the marina. It was sunny, humid. We stepped into a peapod dinghy that barely held the two of us. We had two inches of freeboard, his end sinking heavily into the still water. He was in his midseventies then, still strong, rowing with grunts and concentration. He did not talk. The sailboat was a twenty-eight-foot ketch, dirty white, the cramped cabin sunk with magazines and ashtrays, with hardly a spot to sit or stand. I was polite, trying to say nice things about the boat, which was by then everything he owned, the container of his life. He was able to buy the boat after he and my mother divorced and the house was sold. He had never had an income, except for the last ten years when he worked in a shoe factory, throwing hides onto a stamping machine. He got to keep five dollars a week, which he spent on cigarettes and coffee. The rest he handed over to us, these the only paychecks we saw in twenty-seven years. He had enough money from the sale of the house to buy his boat—to land his dream. I found out later that he couldn't sail it. One trip out of the harbor he had crashed into another boat; the other, the Coast Guard had to tow him back in.

I watched him closely that trip. He had been living on his own for three years by now. Who was he here, now that he was freed from the prison of his family? People who hung out at the marina knew him—the waterfront crowd, most past middle age, long hair, lots of tattoos, some toothless, all inhabiting vessels as wrecked as my father's. Their amazement at my presence was clear. "Who's this, Howard?" they'd asked, in a sly, leering way, like, "You old dog, you!" already reassessing what they thought they knew about him. Of course, no one knew he had children, let alone six of them.

When we ate breakfast in the marina café, the waitress greeted him by name, then asked the same question with open astonishment: "Who is this, Howard?" I watched his face each time someone spoke to him. *Will he look them in the eye?* I wondered. *Does he see them when they speak to him?*

Each time he looked away, or glanced at his questioner and then at me, with the flattened eyes I knew so well. He never said my name. "This is my daughter. She's from Alaska," he would answer with a slight grimace and a mocking tone, his head bobbing slightly.

What little he knew about my life was usually echoed back in this same tone, like a challenge or a joke. "How many kids do you have now?" he might ask at some point, in that same voice. Or, "So you're still fishing, I suppose." Or, "I suppose you still believe in God." Always spoken as if it were an indefensible activity, performed against all sense and reason. My answer never really mattered.

We went to an aquarium, an interest we shared. We both lived on the ocean, the only two in our family of eight. Was this a bond between us? At the aquarium, I would quietly exclaim over a creature. He would come and look with me, but he seldom spoke. We sat outside, eating, no one else there for lunch. I tried to converse, but my efforts were fruitless. My cheer for this outing was failing. How could we sit just two feet from each other, bodies that close, and be so apart? Didn't he remember anything about those years as a family? Didn't he have anything to say about that?

I left after three days of trying to talk and be nice. He hadn't changed.

Later, I searched my memories of him. I remembered him standing in the den when I was nine, his dark suit, his hat, a gray overcoat—the clothes he wore when he drove off every day. A traveling salesman, like his father. But his jobs never lasted for long. He was always fired. My throat caught as he stood there, suitcase in hand. He was leaving, my first memory of his many vanishings. I was sad. He looked so pathetic standing there, my father, and I felt for a moment as though I understood. He and I were the same: we were both locked into something we couldn't escape. It made us weak and small. And it wasn't our fault. I think I hugged him. I may have even cried.

When I was twelve, he took what little was left in the bank and drove off, intending never to return—except we found him one night, his car in the parking lot of a cheap motel two towns away, and made him come back.

He had lived with his parents until he was thirty. He was handsome: dark skin and jet-black hair, perfect features, a muscular body. He had met my mother through a cycling club, the AYH, American Youth Hostels. I do not know how long they knew each other before they married. In the one photo taken after they had just been pronounced husband and wife by a justice of the peace, in front of a few family members, my father's face is blank.

He had wanted to be a writer. At the two-year business college from which he graduated, he was editor of the newspaper. He tested smart, had a high IQ, and spent whatever time he could reading—science and boating magazines, newspapers, and classic novels, a few of which now stand in my own library: *Heart of Darkness*, *The Magic Mountain*, a Charles Dickens anthology. I had read some of his short stories, long hidden in a manila folder. The stories weren't good, but the sentences were long and fluid. He liked words, like I do. When my first book came out, I sent him a copy, but he never answered. I vowed I would never send him another.

Without an income, my mother eventually found some means of provision. Our family work became restoring old colonial houses, most in disrepair, beginning with whatever house we were living in. Following my mother's lead, we labored through weekends, after school, summers, tearing down walls, sanding pine floors, tarring barn roofs, replacing rotten sills. We lived in houses heated with single woodstoves through New Hampshire winters, our rooms below freezing most of the time, and in houses with wells that went dry through the summers. We carried buckets over long fields to wash our clothes. Each time a house was done, we attempted to sell it, though it sometimes took years, our funds from the previous sale dwindling to nothing. My father was there for some of this, the heavy work, but mostly it was us. After hot summer days spent whacking stands of Chinese bamboo with machetes or scraping the dried paint off the massive edifice of the current house, if my father was with us, he was the one who asked my mother for ice cream, an astonishing luxury. We held our breath, awaiting the verdict, and when it was yes, we were glad he had been with us.

My father had fought in the war. His high scores had landed him in navigation school, but he flunked out and was moved to another rank and school. He failed there, too, and with nowhere else to go, he joined the infantry as a foot soldier.

Of his year overseas, he told one story, if asked. He was sitting on top of a tank somewhere in Germany. His fellow soldiers were sitting in the grass, taking a break. Suddenly, he knew he had to get off the tank. He jumped down, and within seconds, a mortar blast hit the tank right where he had been sitting. "So you wouldn't be here today if I hadn't gotten off the tank," he said, in summary, his face expressionless, lips drawn into a line.

"Don't you think that was God?" I remember asking.

"I suppose." He shrugged blandly.

He had been a Christian Scientist for a while, then nothing, then an atheist, with special enthusiasm for UFOs. He watched for them every clear summer night, standing out on the grass and surveying the dark tent overhead. When we were younger, we watched, too, sometimes. He told us of spaceships he had seen, close up, of fireballs shooting at him right there on our back road in New Hampshire—his conversion experience. My siblings would report glimmers of his faith in God now and then, but I never saw him waver from those beliefs.

Except once, twenty years ago. I was living in Anchorage then. A letter with his tight scrawl showed up in my mailbox, the second or third letter he had ever written to me. He had read all the way through the New Testament, he wrote. And he believed in Jesus. Would I forgive him?

I cried bitterly for two days after that letter, because I had had no part to claim in this redemption. I had never even thought to pray for him. And I was not sure I could forgive him: for my invisibility, the poverty, the work, the crises and conflict that raged about him, the nights we hid . . .

A year later, after a flurry of letters between us, he wrote his last letter for a while, tucked inside a box of all the books I had sent him: "Dear Leslie, don't call me Daddy anymore. I am returning all the books you've sent, I don't have room for them on my boat. Don't talk to me about God or church. I'm sending you some magazines you should read." The magazines were full of photos of spaceships and aliens.

I write all this now as remembrance and confession. This is not like some stories of fathers or mothers. It is not horrific. It may be the easiest in this book. But it does not matter how one story measures against another. We're not competing for badges. I write each incident now, though, because it is essential to remember.

I think of Asaph's prayer in Psalm 79: "Do not hold against us the sins of the fathers; may your mercy come quickly to meet us, for we are in desperate need" (v. 8). I think of God's words and warnings to the ancient Hebrews who were stuck in the wilderness:

"Those of you who are left will waste away in the lands of their enemies because of their sins; also because of their fathers' sins they will waste away.

"But if they will confess their sins and the sins of their fathers . . . then when their . . . hearts are humbled . . . I will remember my covenant . . . and I will remember the land." (Lev. 26:39–42)

"But if they will confess . . ." I know a little bit about the word *confession*. It's from the Greek word *homologeo*, meaning "to say the same thing." We are promised by Saint John that if we "confess [*homologeo*] our sins, [God] is faithful and just to forgive us our sins" (1 John 1:9 KJV). When we confess our sins to God, we are attempting to speak the same words about ourselves and our wrongdoing that He does.

When we confess to the sins of our fathers and mothers, our words align with what we have lived, and with what we are experiencing maybe even now. Our words must align with the truth of the world as it is and was, not as we wish it were. We don't always want to do this. We feel like a snake in the garden if we confess that everything's not as it should be. We think we're damaging God's reputation if his own people aren't happy, victorious, and put-together all the time. We don't want to tarnish our own reputations. We don't want to whine and seem weak.

But many writers are not afraid to be confessional. The very ones we think should be the most put-together are quick to cry out, "Where are You, God? How long will You tarry? How long must I wait? My soul faints with longing for You!" David cried out in the Psalms, fully one-third of which begin in such honest lament. Moses penned an almost disturbing psalm (90) that confesses the truth of our experience: "The years of our life are seventy, or even by reason of strength, eighty; yet their span is but toil and trouble; they are soon gone, and we fly away. . . . Return, O LORD! How long? Have pity on your servants! . . . Make us glad for as many days as you have afflicted us" (vv. 10, 13, 15 ESV).

Jesus used words of confession as well, words that invite us to confess the truth. It's a passage most of us know—the sermon on the side of the hill, where Jesus used words that speak blessing, but also words that align with our experience of this life: "Blessed are the *poor in spirit* . . . Blessed are those who *mourn* . . . Blessed are those who *hunger* and *thirst* for righteousness . . . Blessed are those who are *persecuted*" (Matt. 5:3–6, 10; emphasis added).

These are words that express the very real conditions of our lives.

Confession. Daring to confess. We can confess lesser things too. Not all is sorrow and neglect.

Daniel's father would come home from work, pick up the newspaper by the front door, and enter Daniel's world with his face in the news. Daniel would run to him and then wait for him to tear away his eyes from the paper before he hugged him.

Tina's mother would never pick her up when she needed a ride home after baseball practice, even though it was a two-and-a-half-mile walk home.

Brandon's father traveled a lot for his job, so he missed most of Brandon's concerts and basketball games.

Shannon's mother, who struggled with her weight, refused to cook for her family, so Shannon cooked, or they ate cereal for dinner.

And then harder things.

Jeanne's father was a minister. He stood up in front of pews of people, preaching the Bible while Jeanne sat glowering, knowing her father was a jerk. He railroaded the congregants into doing whatever he wanted them to do, and it was far worse at home. His arrogance closed him off to others, especially his children. Jeanne grew up afraid of him. When she was sexually abused by a neighbor, he refused to believe it and did nothing.

After Molly's mother died, she found herself both grieving and fighting with her brother over her mother's estate. One night she unexpectedly fell apart. She and her husband met with a friend who was a counselor, and with his encouragement, she began journaling, confessing the sins committed against her as a child. Every day, remembering, she wrote about her mom and her dad. She wrote about not feeling wanted by either one. She always felt lost among them, invisible. She knew her father wasn't well, that he was emotionally disturbed. He threw fits of rage in public, oblivious to those around them. Molly wrote about her parents' affairs, their anger, their dysfunction, even her mother's inappropriate confessions to her. She wrote that she knew she was not wanted. Her parents had forsaken her. She wrote about her suppressed anger and unforgiveness, how much she resented both mother and father.

She journaled every day, remembering, confessing.

We can no longer be silent about these events. We take courage as we speak, because of Christ's own life. L. Gregory Jones, noted professor of theology at Duke Divinity School, reminds us in his excellent book *Embodying Forgiveness: A Theological Analysis* that we do not call out to an untested Savior. "If Christians claim to worship not Christ *un*crucified but Christ crucified and risen, then we of all people ought to know that the past can be borne in hope—even if it takes a lifetime to learn how to do so well."[2]

The past *can* be borne in hope . . .

The story Vonnie has committed to writing for her son—she told me some of it the night after the aforementioned seminar, and then much more in a phone call later. These are some of the most disturbing words from a childhood that I have heard. It is hard to even include them here, but I do, because this happened. Because I know her. Because it is only how her story begins. It is not how it ends. There is so much more that will follow. But she begins here, confessing:

We lived in the woods. My father was gone a lot. But whenever he came home, I was terrified. I planned my whole day around staying away from him. If he was inside, I would go outside. I would try not to sit next to him at the dinner table. I tried to stay home if he wanted to go somewhere. I don't remember my name even being used. He called me "waitress" all the time. Or "dummy." If his coffee cup was empty, he'd yell. All of us kids were at risk, but it seemed to happen to me most, because I was the oldest. It would start with yelling and move into peeling off his belt; then he'd fold it in half and crack it, make that snapping noise, and then just come after us. We never tried to run. It would be a lot worse [if we did]. If the other kids weren't dressed right, he'd come after me. One of the worst things he would do is strip me down. One time when I was ten, and my sister was a toddler and had been running in a diaper, she had stepped out of her diaper. He came after me and punished me for that by making me strip down, naked below the waist. He had some buddies that were over, and he made me serve them drinks naked. He really enjoyed my misery.

He would pick me up and bring me into his bedroom, and I don't remember anything, just coming out of the door. I was diagnosed a few years ago with DID, disassociative identity disorder, because I've had occasions off and on even as an adult where I just kind of check out. I went to counseling for many years.

My mother asked me to kill him when I was twelve years old. If she did it, she would go to jail. But if I did it, since I was a child, I wouldn't go to jail. She told me and my sister, showed us the gun. Loaded. If we waited until midnight, we could go in and sneak in and shoot him.

There was a lot of torment in my house.

We've run away from all of this and sometimes made a mess of our lives in the running. Now we are slowing, stopping, daring to turn back and remember, not because we are selfish or masochistic or victim junkies, but because we have not abandoned hope for justice and rightness in this world. We know that parents are supposed to act like mothers and fathers and do fatherly and motherly things. And even when the whole world seems bent against what is right and pure and good, we hold out for its presence. We say the same words that God does about the sins visited upon us. We abhor the wrongs; we confess the wrongs. We remember now all that was done, because we will not know the right until we acknowledge the wrong.

And we confess as well the shattering of our own dreams. Where is the happy life we hoped we would have? Life, liberty, and the pursuit of happiness—our national genetic code—weren't passed down to us. And if we are Christians, raised in the church, our expectations for a happy family life are even higher. The shattering, then, pierces all the sharper.

I am not done acknowledging the wrong. A few years ago, Laurie, my other sister Jan, and I were together for five days in

South Carolina. We were all staying in a rented condo. One night Laurie and I stayed up, and the talk turned to our father. There were things to be said, and the time was short. Laurie got down to business right away.

"Dad used to come into my room," she told me.

I stared at her. She was sitting in the corner, her face composed, one of the most beautiful fifty-three-year-old women I ever knew. I was struck dumb. My stomach heaved. I felt my face go hot and red with anger.

"What? What do you mean? How often?" I was fixed, unbreathing.

"Whenever he could. For many years. That's why I would run away at night."

"What?"

Silence.

"*What?*" I didn't know what else to say. I felt like the stupidest person on earth. How could I not have known?

"Why didn't you tell me?" I was angry at her now, at her silence all these years. Only *now* I was finding out, after all this time, that my father had been sexually abusing my sister for most of her childhood?

"Laurie, why didn't you tell me?"

"What would you have done, Leslie? There was nothing you could have done."

I was wild with anger and sorrow. "I don't know, but I wouldn't have allowed it! I would have made him stop! I could have!" I thought back to my ten- and twelve-year-old self. I thought of my determination that had powered me through so much in my own life. I was sure I could have stopped him. I was strong. I did push-ups and pull-ups every day. I would have fought him, hit him with

a bat, anything. I imagined it, fighting this enemy. He was heavy
and muscular. He belted us hard with his leather strap when we
disobeyed, but he could never hurt me, and I was not afraid of
him. Even as I talked to my sister, I had the sense that I could
reach back forty years and stop the sexual abuse, with my own
long, strong arms and with the fire of innocence and sisterly
protection.

My sister, my beautiful sister, whose life had been so hard, and
now I knew why. I finally knew why.

We sat for a few minutes. Laurie was calm. Finally I asked what
I didn't want to know, but I had to. I could not let it pass. *She must
say it. I must listen. It must be spoken,* I thought.

"What did he do, Laurie?"

And she told me. I did not cry, but there was reason to. It
wasn't the worst—but it was ugly and sick. And I realized it was
her instead of me. It was her instead of our other sister. I knew
instantly it was true.

"He tried with me, too, you know."

"Yeah, I think I knew that. What did he do?"

I told her.

Laurie nodded calmly.

We sat for a few minutes in silence. I didn't remember ever
talking about this before, but we must have over the years. It was
not news. But it was still confession, and we were saying it out loud
to each other for the first time. It wasn't pleasant. But it had to be
said and faced.

"Dad ruined my life, you know?" Laurie said evenly.

I nodded.

———

I would not have guessed that two years later, my sister and I would be renting another condo, this time in Florida, to see our father, just the two of us. We were thousands of miles away from home, spending a lot of money to be there, to sit beside this man while he ate his chicken and pears in the dining room.

We took his arm and shuffled with him down the hall back to his room. We smiled and we were kind. We acted as though this man, our father, had been kind and good to us, and that we were repaying a debt.

When the visit began, my heart kept sinking. I thought of Jonah thrown overboard, flailing as he plunged into the deep, arms twining in the kelp, feet running futile under water. I did not love mercy just then. I did not even like it. We were still confessing, still unraveling a lifetime of absence from a father, and a lifetime of presence in all the wrong ways.

"Those of you who are left will waste away in the lands of their enemies . . . because of their fathers' sins . . . But if they will confess their sins and the sins of their fathers . . . then when their . . . hearts are humbled . . . I will remember my covenant" (Lev. 26:39–42).

This is the truth of our experience. There will be more truths along the way, but without these, there is no place to start. We have run, and we have stopped and dared to leap into the sea of confession and remembrance. Like Jonah, we cannot bear the thought of mercy—those people! The carnage they've brought! The unspeakable things they have done! Even the ordinary faults of mothers and fathers—the gall of it, the bitterness it brings, all that was taken from us as sons and daughters. These waters are cold; we cannot breathe. We may be here for just a few moments, or we may be here longer. But we will move on. Jonah would have drowned without a rescue, without entrance into the safety of further truths. So will we. We've lost so much, but if we stay here, we'll lose what's left.

We can become fully ourselves again, fully alive, fully human. So many have done it before us. It is our turn now.

AFTERWORD . . . WITH DR. JILL

Confession . . . courage . . . truth.

Have you ever wondered why certain people who have hor-rendous life stories appear to rise above their pain, while others with comparatively milder sorrows endlessly struggle and anguish? The truth is, hurt and suffering are not doled out according to magnitude of story. There is no hierarchy for misfortune, dysfunc-tion, or tragedy. There are seemingly random acts of devastation, completely out of our control . . . and there are also deliberate, almost compulsive acts of cruelty (like those of Vonnie's father) that can only be labeled as evil.

I think of the young woman waiting to make a left turn at a signal in my hometown. It was a sunny, wind-free September after-noon. School was out, and hordes of kids (my daughter included) invaded the nearby convenience store for after-school snacks. To their shock and horror, they witnessed a scurry of rescue workers trying to free this woman from her crushed vehicle. There was no explanation. More than a hundred eucalyptus trees lined that stretch of road, and on that day and at that moment, one ten-ton, fifty-foot tree just fell over and crushed her to death. She was a twenty-nine-year-old accomplished violinist who had even played at Carnegie Hall and was now running a training center for kids. Why, Lord, did someone who added so much fall prey to this ran-dom tragedy?

Life's randomness underscores our limited capacity for con-trol. One stormy winter eve, I arrived home to find it literally raining in our family room. How could this happen? Our couch, tables, rug, and wood flooring were drenched and practically floating. It had been an unusually heavy rain season, and after investigation, problems were found with our construction. The builders we had trusted had not properly assessed what the future would bring. Our house looked beautiful, but cracks below the well-covered surface could not hold up when put to the test. What seemed like a random event was actually quite predictable, had we been aware of the construction flaws.

No matter the reason, I was left with the damage and the cleanup. So it is with our emotional lives as well. Family dysfunctions are not random—they are fairly predictable. The sins of our fathers and mothers are acts, attitudes, afflictions that affect each child differently and not evenly. Siblings raised in the same environment often report different perspectives concerning the same experience. Personality type, disposition, age, and degree of exposure—all play into outcome and impact.

Some kids handle family dysfunction by acting out. They become the ones who externalize the family pain, often compounding their already difficult lives. Others "act in"—they internalize their pain and so appear to be okay. They are peacemakers instead of pot stirrers. But don't be fooled. The "good child" rarely escapes childhood scar-free.

When sin is not brought into relationship with the One who can free us from that sin, hearts and hurts remain unchanged. When there is no awareness, acknowledgment, surrender, confession, remorse, or repentance, there is a very predictable runoff that spills over from one generation to the next.

Knowingly and unknowingly, parents often damage their children. Sometimes, well-intentioned fathers or mothers do harm because they simply know no better. At the other end of the spectrum are parents who cannot contain their own internal struggles and instead release them unfettered on their children. At either end of the damage scale, or at any shade of gray in between, children eventually come of age. At some point they pass just mere survival and must face the hard, sometimes ugly truth and clean up the mess.

God has given us amazing brains that work to protect and preserve us during times of unimaginable stress. Vonnie suffered from dissociative identity disorder, or DID (historically known as multiple personality disorder). Traumatic, repeating events can reach a level of intensity where a person's mind can't comprehend or tolerate the internal dissonance of what is happening. When there is no escape, as a means of literal survival, our brains can send us into shock or a state of dissociation. DID compartmentalizes these memories into split-off feeling states, like rooms in a house where doors are shut to hide the clutter; our brains shut the door on certain experiences until we are safe and ready to clean house.

Until we name what has happened or is happening, we cannot get the perspective we need to move through it. *I once was blind but now I see* (John 9:25, 39)—until we share the truth, out loud, to another, it's hard to truly see it. Admitting to ourselves "the exact nature of our wrongs," as stated by the twelve steps of AA—or the *wrongs done* to *us*—is a good start. Certainly, crying out to God is healing. It's not as though God is unaware of your past. Psalm 56:8 says,

> You keep track of all my sorrows.
> You have collected all my tears in your bottle.
> You have recorded each one in your book. (NLT)

That we should keep things "just between me and God" is the life-halting lie our shame tells us. Confession to and connection with others is powerful and essential. We must realize we can't go it alone. God sent us His Son in human form so we could more easily relate. He wants us to be in relationship, to "share each other's burdens" (Gal. 6:2 NLT). When we cry with others, we allow ourselves to be comforted, and "God blesses those who mourn, for they will be comforted" (Matt. 5:4 NLT).

Confession takes courage—courage to speak the truth out loud, just as Laurie and Leslie did. They shared, they cried, they comforted . . . but they also had to be specific. It's not enough to vaguely allude. When we teach a child to apologize to a friend, "I'm sorry for what I did wrong" doesn't cut it. The child must name the wrong to have it sink in. The same principle is needed for us as well. We must confess how we've been hurt. Unfortunately, there is no getting around our pain; we must go through it to get to the other side—where true freedom exists.

Study Questions

1. What are the predominant feelings you had growing up with your father or mother, or both?
2. Describe a childhood memory with your father or mother where you had these feelings.
3. What are the predominant feelings you have with your father or mother today?
4. If you could share freely with your father or mother, without fear of retribution, what would you want your parent to know about you?
5. What new awareness could you add to your childhood story, as an adult, that you didn't know or couldn't have known growing up?

6. Were there any other significant adults during your childhood who offered comfort, refuge, or help in bearing your childhood burdens?

7. Read John 9:35–41. What does it mean to be spiritually blind? Especially considering verse 39, what impact does Jesus' statement have on you?

8. Are there additional issues from the ways you have coped that also need to be confessed?

9. If you are a parent, do you see repetitions of some of the ways you were parented reflected in the parenting of your own kids?

10. In what ways have you made different choices with your children from how your father or mother parented you?

Becoming Human:
The Debt We Share

How did I get so lucky to have my heart awakened to others and their sufferings?

—Pema Chodron[1]

The line dividing good and evil cuts through the heart of every human being.

—Aleksandr Solzhenitsyn[2]

Remember our reluctant prophet from chapter 1? We know what happens to our man Jonah next. This is the fantastical part of the story, when a giant fish gulps him whole, landing him alive, barely, in its belly. It's not much of a rescue. Why not a simple life preserver or a convenient desert island? But Jonah's a hard case. He refuses to see himself; his confessions of sin are scant and slanted. He's so blinded by the Ninevites, his enemies, that he refuses to wrestle with a truth larger and nearer: his own bent toward sin. His own hard heart. His own refusal to offer forgiveness. Jonah misses essential truths in his haste for rescue—and we will, too, in our own quests to forgive our parents, if we don't attend to further realities.

We'll leave him there, then. He cannot instruct us where we need to go next. Our starting place in this book for naming and understanding sin has begun with those who have sinned against us. We know how heinous sin is. We have felt its corrosion in our very hearts and flesh. We know that, in the words of Eugene Peterson,

> Sin kills. Sin kills relationships. Sin kills the soul-intimacy that is inherent in the image-of-God creature that we are. Sin is deadly, summarized in the "seven deadly sins." Part of us dies when we sin, no longer in a living relation with the living God, the living spouse, the living child, the living neighbor. . . . Daily we find ourselves walking through this vast sin cemetery of what someone has described as the "undead dead."[3]

But we are far enough along now to consider something larger than what's been done to us. I know we hunger, all of us, for relief from our anger and our pain. We long for justice. All of this is warranted. But I know we hunger just as passionately for the truth, for truths that are larger than us. We want to be affirmed in our pain, but there is another pull—to see beyond ourselves and the pain that has locked us in an isolation chamber and numbed us to the larger world.

We will go there now, stepping back from our own stories, to consider our parents' stories. Maybe we haven't done this at all yet—seen more fully into our mothers' and fathers' lives, who they are as people apart from the harm they've done to us. This is not easy to do. We can barely see into ourselves with any clarity.

We often have an even greater blindness toward our parents. For lots of reasons. We may not want to take the time to see into their hearts and their histories. We've kept a distance from them. We don't want to see similarities, parallels between us and them. We want to be utterly different from them. As I've interviewed others, I hear it again and again: "The best my parents gave me was to show me what *not* to do. I don't want to be anything like them."

I'm certain you're *not* like them. But I want to step back, then, for a few moments to gain a larger view of who our parents are—and finally, a larger view of ourselves.

To do this may cost us some phone calls. Some visits. Some travel. Before I took my family to see my father in Sarasota, we drove to St. Petersburg to visit his brother, his only living relative. This was my one chance to ask the questions I was just starting to ask. Who was this man? Why was he so numb and distant? Was it someone's fault, and if so, whose? I considered possible answers to this. It was our fault, the six of us kids. We were too much responsibility. We were too much noise and demand and expense. In one of his short stories, squirreled away in an old manila folder, my father wrote of a young man walking on the beach. His wife and young children are far from him. He hears them all calling him, and his feet grow heavy in the sand. He is rooted and cannot move toward them.

It could be his parents' fault. I had heard stories already, how his mother had favored his brother: garrulous, handsome, witty, popular, at the center of friends and activities. My father was movie-star handsome but nothing else. Maybe his mother had done it, so crushed him that he withdrew from everyone. I knew he didn't like his mother very much. Maybe it was his father, whom he resembled in looks. While growing up, his father had taken him on sales trips—he was a traveling salesman. He had his own business, importing and distributing wool. Had he hoped his son would take over the business? But my father must have been a keen disappointment. He was nothing but a disaster at selling. He couldn't meet his father's expectations.

Was it marriage that crushed him? The demands of a daily relationship he couldn't fulfill? I had recognized how little my mother received from him as a husband—perhaps nothing? But I had not considered his end of the contract.

If I could find out what he was like as a child . . . Had we all done some violence to his gentle soul to make him the way he was? Perhaps I would find some answers with my aunt and uncle, my only remaining aunt and uncle, whom I hadn't seen since I left home thirty years before.

They were in their mideighties then and invited us into their apartment with a mix of astonishment and warmth. After all the pleasantries and news of the last thirty years, I nudged Duncan and the kids outside so I could talk with my aunt and uncle alone. I asked them every question I could think of: What was my father like as a boy? Did he have many friends? What was his mother like? What did he like to do? Did he change over the years? The answers, given hesitantly and always skewed to the positive when possible, did not surprise me. He was a loner. He liked reading and would disappear with a book for hours. When his brother's friends came over to play football, he would escape so he wouldn't have to play. He didn't talk much.

About his time in the army during World War II, my aunt told me brightly, "Your father was a hero!" But nothing else supports this claim. Though his high test scores landed him in navigation school, as I mentioned earlier, he flunked out. Then he was moved to another division, to clerical work, but he failed at that also. Finally he landed in the infantry, a foot soldier. They were embarrassed as they told me this. They also told me they'd visited him a year ago, and his teeth were just about all gone and he had gotten fat. His clothes were dirty. I would be shocked. Maybe the children shouldn't see him, my aunt suggested.

I listened closely, watching their faces. Despite my aunt's very kind attempt to rehabilitate my father's history, I heard it clearly: Failure. At every step. His family was embarrassed by him. As were we. Growing up, we did not respect him. He was berated. There were violent fights, with household furnishings smashed or turned to weapons. There was blood sometimes, words painted on the walls, the house shaking on its foundations, and screaming, accusing voices and words.

Then his work. He was trying to sell burglar alarms. He was trying to sell lingerie from a trunk. He was trying to sell steel buildings. Then at some point no one wanted to hire him anymore. Nor would his brother keep taking him in when he had to leave our house. Nor did we want him anymore ourselves.

When we staged a family reunion, ten years after I left home, we wondered how he was. No one had seen or heard from him in years, but we knew he was in Florida, living on a sailboat. My brother Todd drove from New Hampshire to Florida to pick him up—my father didn't have a car—and drove him all the way back, a four-thousand-mile round-trip. And he sat among his children and grandchildren uncomfortably, nearly silent.

I was determined to get something out of that visit with him: I made him hold my firstborn. He refused at first, but I handed her to him with some unnamed hope that he would fall in love with her. That he would melt and become a grandfather for a few moments.

He took her, held her stiffly on his lap, then quickly gave her back, dangling her from her armpits as if handing off a dirty puppy. Soon after, he left us all in the living room to sit in another room, alone.

I saw it, finally. He is not loved. And he himself will not—or cannot—love. And I was not angry this time.

"What is hell?" Father Zossima asks in *The Brothers Karamazov*. "It is the suffering of being unable to love."[4]

Who has suffered worse? I wondered. I knew the answer.

It was not until my life was more than half over that I cared or even dared to see this: my siblings and I were not the only ones lying wounded on the side of the road.

I could not help but think of an old, old story. Most of us know the story well. Here is its simplest retelling:

A man travels down from one city to another on a road known for being dangerous. Along the way he is mugged, beaten, stripped, robbed, and left for dead beside the road.

A priest passes by, a professional spiritual leader, who is the first person we expect to stop and help. He does not.

A Levite comes next, an expert in the law (like the one questioning Jesus in Luke 10:25–29) who knows what God asks of him. He ignores God's law and this man, continuing blithely on his way.

A third man comes, from Samaria, a people despised, considered half-breeds, and deemed a threat to the purity of the Jewish nation and their religion. He, the least likely, is the one who stops and binds up the stranger's wounds, loads him on his own donkey, and houses him at an inn, where he leaves money for his food and lodging. He even comes back later to check on this man he does not know.

We recognize the first of this story. Isn't it about us? There we are! We start out, fresh and innocent, down the road. It's a long

trip, from the cities of our birth to the other city down in the valley. We are so naive and new that we don't even know about the
dangers ahead. Everyone walks this road from childhood to adult.
What harm could come?

It is not long before it happens. From behind the rocks,
through the darkest part of the valley, our assailants jump us. They
steal our valuables, strip us of our clothes, and beat us, and we are
there, bleeding, helpless, our journey interrupted—maybe ended
altogether. People walk by, people who know they should stop and
help, but they don't. We are left there alone, in pain. Do you see
yourself in this story?

I see myself, and I see Michelle, literally lying on the floor,
knocked out. She was in high school, and had started into alcohol
and drugs. And her father had hit her—again.

The pattern was well established. Michelle would come home
late at night, drunk, and her father, furious, would punch her in
the face and knock her out. He would stand over her, kicking at
her, until she came to. He had so much anger. There were nine
kids in the family, five teenagers at once, but all his rage came
down on her, "the black sheep," the name—among others—that
he used for her. Michelle would run away to downtown Buffalo,
wild, feeling completely lost in her own anger. She told anyone
who would listen, "I'm done with my dad! I'm done with all this!"

Michelle remained there in that position, bleeding beside the
road, for fifteen years.

It's easy to see ourselves as the one fallen beside the road. We
like how the parable ends for him. Yes, he's the one who is violated, but eventually he's the one who is tended to, who is finally
lifted tenderly and carried to the inn, where his needs are met
and cared for. He heals, is restored to full health. That's what we

want for ourselves, to be cared for and tended back to health. This happened for Michelle. But it didn't happen by itself. It happened because of her own realizations and actions.

She began to realize that we are not the only ones who started out on that road and were jumped from behind. Our mothers—our fathers too—started off in hope. They, too, were unprepared for the dangers that lay ahead. They, too, were unsuspecting, not knowing they were entering such danger. When we begin to look at them again, even if we can only lift our heads, we can see they are there as well, bleeding, weak. They are as human, as fully human, and likely as wounded as we are.

When her sister died tragically and Michelle went home to be with her family, she looked across the room one day and saw her father there, suffering as deeply as she was.

> He was like a ghost to me for fifteen years—and then he was this real human being. I started to look more and more to my own culpability. Which brought me to my appropriate stature. I used to see him as guilty, and I started seeing myself as more guilty. I was drunk all those times he hit me. I started to see I had a role to play in all of that. He didn't have any better equipment to use than I did to understand it all. Yes, I was drowning, but so was he. My father was under extraordinary pain. He had four other daughters in great trouble. I watched him age rapidly. He was fading away.
>
> When I took the time to look closer and tried to see our family through his eyes—I realized there were so many things going on in our lives. I can't believe how he held the family together. I saw him floundering. Lonely, the pain. We had financial issues, and the house was up for sale because of it. He was amazing. . . .

Suddenly I get this whole perspective that helped me tremen-
dously. I didn't know much about him. I didn't know he had
wanted to be a sailor his whole life. He loved plants and was a
skillful gardener. He wanted to start a nursery. I hadn't known
that. It dawned on me [that] he had sacrificed thirty years of his
life for his family. He had arthritis, lost his hearing at the Chevy
plant. He worked so hard. His foibles and sins and guilt are very
small compared to what I once thought they were.

It almost feels enough at this point to leave ourselves in this
parable lying close enough to our parents to see them there, but
the hopeful ending, and the identity of the Samaritan, involves us
in another way.

Yes, you've heard this story a thousand times before, but look
again. The Jewish victim was far worse than a stranger to the man
from Samaria: he was actually related. The Samaritans shared
ancestral history. The Hebrews were slaves under Pharaoh and were
delivered by Moses, but later, the kingdom they went on to form
split into the Northern and Southern kingdoms. The Samaritans
in the Northern Kingdom fell captive to the Assyrians in 722 B.C.
and eventually intermarried with their captors and other Arabian
colonists, despite God's prohibition against it. They grew distant
from their fellow Hebrews in the Southern Kingdom. The Jews
came to hate and denounce the Samaritans and their claim to
the Jewish faith. Samaritans could not serve as witnesses in Jewish
courts. Samaritans were publicly cursed in the synagogues. The
Jews believed they would be contaminated just by crossing their
borders. Samaritans weren't even allowed to convert to Judaism.
Without a doubt, that Samaritan man and his entire family and
culture had suffered much from the Jews. And here was a Jewish

man, lying at his feet. He had far more reasons to refuse to see him, to refuse to help, than did the two men, fellow countrymen, before him.

But he looked past the injustices and his own hurts and their own tangled history and saw all that bound them: he was a fellow traveler; he was taken advantage of. He was helpless to help himself. The Samaritan man knew exactly how that felt. He saw the fallen man for who he was most purely and truly in that moment: a man who would die without his help, a neighbor.

We are here in this story more than once. Here's what I find. We're still the victim in this story—there's little doubt—but we're not entirely off the hook here. Even if you feel rejected or cast out by your parents, even if you've worn the label "black sheep," if your situation is that severe—that makes *you* a Samaritan. And that means you are asked to do as he did to the very one who afflicted him—according to your ability, as God gives strength.

Here is what happened with Michelle: She and her father were slowly reconciled. Her father became real and alive to her. They began exchanging small gifts. When she was in the Coast Guard, she brought him a gift, a Coast Guard ship belt buckle. The words were hard to say, but she brought it to him to say, "Thank you for sacrificing your dreams for your family."

After she gave him the gift, she was on her way back to the ship. When she got into her car, she said, "I love you," something she hadn't said for a very long time. Then he reached his hand in the window, pressed it to her face, held her cheek for a few seconds, and said, "I love you too." It was the first time he had touched her lovingly since she was young. Michelle rolled up her window, drove until she was out of his sight, then parked and sobbed.

She saw him one more time, a few years later, in August. She had a good visit. When she went back to the barracks, he had put a tiny television in her backpack as a gift. She was going to call him the next day to thank him. He died of a heart attack that next morning.

Michelle remembers most the last touch on her face and the gift her father had stuffed in her pack. When she got to her father's house, before they removed his body, she saw he was wearing the belt buckle she had given him years before.

Michelle was able to see her father clearly and to go to his side. Others have moved across the road to stand, or kneel, beside their parents too.

———————

Diana avoided her mother most of her adult life. She never knew what to do with her behavior. Her mom would cut off communication with her whenever she did something to displease her, sometimes for years at a time. There were affairs, suicide attempts. Diana cannot recall many happy memories; their large family reeled constantly from the turmoil of her mother's decisions.

Eventually, as Diana began to examine her mother's childhood, she slowly began to put the pieces together and realized her mother had likely been sexually abused as a child. She began to develop sympathy for her mother and saw in her suicide attempt and her stays at rehab facilities efforts to deal with her past. No one tried to help her deal with the abuse. Her mother still will not speak of her growing-up years, but Diana sees her lying beside the road.

Sympathy. It's a leaning forward, a turn of the head, a courageous look across the road, the room.

Andy's parents were both alcoholics. He tells me of growing up with beatings, constant insults, and disparagement. His place at the table was by his father's right hand, which meant he was back-handed onto the floor with regularity when his father was mad. His mother was a thrower and would heave whatever was handiest at her son: a cup of hot coffee, once a bucket of boiling water. I could not record the wounds fast enough as he talked, but the story he told me was not just about him. He told, too, about his mother's background. She was an only child who had no idea how to raise five kids. His father grew up fatherless and left home at fourteen, essentially raising himself. "I can cut him a lot of slack," Andy said. "He had no way of knowing how to raise a kid."

When I talked to Caroline on the phone about her parents, she began with their history, not with hers. With their life circumstances. Where they lived, their politics, who their parents were. How they were hurt. I was astonished as I listened to her, knowing that even though she still struggles with forgiveness, she sees them. She sees them as fellow human beings suffering under the weight of their own inheritances.

It is not a simple thing to do this, to see beyond the roles our mothers and fathers at least partially failed at. To see beyond our need for them to their larger selves. But they were always more than our mothers and fathers. If you have children yourself, you know the truth of this, how much our children don't know about us. How much of ourselves we hold back. Don't we know that our own parents were boys and girls, with parents themselves and siblings and a kitchen sink with a leaky faucet and a sickly brother and a teacher they disliked and a secret hideout in their attic? And if they married, they did so with dreams and hopes for good lives, better lives than they were given in their own first homes. And when your mother birthed you, she may have wept with joy. And if she gave you to someone else, to another set of parents, she may have wept with grief. Your father may remember the day you were born as the best day of his life.

They are more like us than we imagine, likely more than we care to admit. Beyond the physical resemblances, the similar voice inflections, the shared DNA, the household, the family tree, the obligations, histories, and memories, we share some things with our parents that are even deeper: We are pressed alike in the inescapable fist of time. We alike are made of humus, the dirt of the earth, and to dirt we alike will return. We alike are under bondage to ourselves, and we share a nature bent away from God. We alike are sharers in "the universal disaster of sinful brokenness."[5] It is probable that our parents were harmed by their parents. As people hurt by our parents, we likely have gone on to hurt our own family members around us. We could, then, all of us, sons and daughters, mothers and fathers, pray together Eugene Peterson's words:

> Forgive us our debts. Forgive us for our failure to keep honest accounts with our neighbors. Forgive us for refusing the gifts that are given and stealing what is not ours to have. Forgive us for using the gift of language to deceive. Forgive us for using the gift of sexuality to seduce. Forgive us for using the gift of strength to abuse and murder. Forgive us for using the gift of plenty to impoverish another.[6]

But we're not stuck here. We're also made alike in the image of God, containing the very breath of God in our lungs. We each long for freedom, for a life that matters. We are equally the recipients of God's love and mercy. We all are offered a new life, redemption, the removal of sins, the hope of heaven, the company of God's Spirit within us. We share with our parents both in this "universal disaster of sinful brokenness"[7] and in the universal offer of wholeness and restoration.

I am not suggesting you share fault or guilt in what happened during your childhood. Most of us were not complicit in our parents' failures when we were children living under their roofs. But we are no longer children. We no longer live under their roofs. Who are we now? Who are *they* now?

We must not be afraid to look, and to look closely. Not to excuse them, or ourselves. None of this is about excusing sin. It's not for us to excuse. God does not excuse sin, does not just wipe it away with a knowing wink, a nod to our earthen frames, sweeping our human humus under the rug of His largesse. Sin and harm and evil must be dealt with completely. Not ignored or denied or excused away. Excusing your parents is not forgiving your parents. Don't patronize them by relieving them of responsibility. If they are merely excused, there is no opportunity for them to acknowledge their responsibility, to repent, to seek forgiveness, to move away from the habits and wrongs of the past to another kind of living and relating to people. And you will continue to carry the full weight of their actions, with little relief or resolution, while they continue to bear the guilt of their offenses. We won't be satisfied with this fake forgiveness. We're after something much more.

During the last year of my father's life, he had a stroke. I was in Santa Fe, New Mexico, that night, in a fancy restaurant with colleagues and friends. After dinner we were all going to a keynote lecture by a well-known writer. I was going to introduce her. In the middle of laughter and deepening conversation, my cell phone rang. It was my sister. Within a minute I was pacing an empty corner of the restaurant, tears running, voice cracking, hands running through my hair, as I heard the details of his fall, how long he lay on the floor without help, how helpless he had become, where he had finally been taken. We were convulsed with anger at the negligence that kept our father from getting help sooner and broken with pity as we envisioned the events unfolding. It occurred to me even then how costly this new relationship was. His fall and stroke hurt so much more now that I cared about him.

My sister flew to be with him a few days later. I wanted to meet her there, but I had been teaching for two weeks already and had to return home. Duncan had to leave on an essential business trip, and I needed to be there with the kids. And isn't this how it happens, a parent dying in the middle of your life when your family at home still needs you? Is there ever a good time to have a stroke?

During her visit, Laurie held the phone up to his ear so I could talk to him.

"Hi, Dad. This is Leslie, in Alaska."

He exclaimed with surprise. Then I heard just heavy breathing.

"I just wanted to call and let you know I am praying for you every day. Did you get my card?"

He made a sound—I'm not sure what it was.

"I know it's frustrating, that you have the words in your head, but you can't speak them."

"Frust—" he echoed painfully.

"I sent a card and then a book to you. Does someone bring your mail to you and then read it to you?"

I heard a heavy grunting that I think was affirmative.

"Oh, good. I'm glad you got it. Dad, I heard that Clark was there to see you. He's moved down to Florida, and he plans to see you every week or two. And I'll be seeing you in about three weeks!" I tried to make my voice cheerful, to lift him from his misery. To infuse some kind of joy into his life.

"I'mmm . . . not . . . worth . . . ," he stumbled.

Then I realized with a stab in my gut what he was saying. "Of *course* you're worth it!" I protested, horrified. But I knew instantly what he meant. In the human balances of justice and fairness, he had done nothing to earn or deserve this kind of sacrifice and attention from his children. We were giving up huge chunks of time, giving up money some of us didn't have. One brother sold his home and moved two thousand miles to be near him. We were putting our lives on hold for him. He was the one who chose to live half a country away from us. He was right. He was entirely right about this. Every time I had turned toward him during the last year, I was acutely aware that whatever I was doing for him had not been done for me. Yet hearing those words from his own halting tongue, I immediately knew in my deepest self that the universe did not work that way. His words violated the very grain of the universe—a universe made out of the fullness of love, out of unmeasured mercy—that every person is God-made and God-breathed and deserves attention and kindness. No man, no woman, no parent left behind.

That next week, Duncan returned from his trip, so I was free now to go. I flew down from Kodiak to be with him, just the two of us. He was in a rehab facility by then. I flew into Orlando, rented a car, and drove to the facility, wondering who I would find, what would be left. The last time I'd seen him, a few months before, he'd had all his faculties. He'd walked painfully slowly with a walker, but he was upright and cogent, though he never said much.

This time, I inched down the hallway as I approached his room. I peered around the doorway and saw it was a room for two. A figure lay curled on the bed, and then, through a half-open curtain, I saw another man in a wheelchair. I entered tremulously.

My father was lying on his side, curled knees to chest. He was wearing shorts. His jaw hung open, all his teeth gone now. He was much thinner, yet his legs were solid still, muscular. *What do I do? What do I know about this—visiting the sick, the elderly, a father?* I felt as if I was supposed to know, but I didn't. *Do I wait?* I had come five thousand miles, and my time was short. I didn't want to wait. I inched closer to the bed, deciding . . . yes, I would wake him, if possible.

I touched his shoulder through the thin jersey, lightly, and watched his face. I held my fingers there for a moment, and he blinked; then his eyes opened. He looked directly at me without moving his head. Seeing me, his eyes filled with tears and, still looking, he began to weep, a silent, shaking weeping, his whole body shuddering as he sobbed, his head still lying on his hands. I stood frozen for a moment. I had never seen my father weep—or even teary or sad. I was torn in half. My face crumpled. I kept my hand on his shoulder to comfort his racking body, and there we were, bodies touching, both shaking in silent sobs, our faces lost in sadness and grief. I knew he could not speak or name the sorrows that shook him, but it seemed to me we wept, the two of us, for his life, for his long, sad life, for his breaking body, his tangled mind, and a tongue that was now nearly stilled. I cried that I had not seen him sooner. We were crying for all that was lost to us both.

Later, I could not but wonder at this: the stroke, the sickness, had rendered him more fully human than I had ever seen him. I had not expected this: I saw my father through eyes of mercy and kindness. And I was sad as well.

Did it really take a stroke to render him worthy of pathos?

———

We have gained a little more vantage from this vie
now at whatever terrain separates you from yo
mother, your mother-in-law, your stepfather, even
ent. Is it possible that someone is there on the other side of the
road, someone like you—stripped, knocked out, unable even to
ask for help? Might that person be the wounded also?

I am not insisting that as you look you feel a flood of emotion,
as I did in those moments. I am not even insisting on warm feelings. Instead I am inviting perspective.

As you look into your parents' lives, consider the words of Jesus
on the cross, perhaps the most shocking words ever uttered, as He
struggled for breath, His body so bloodied He was nearly unrecognizable as a man. He had done no evil, no wrong at all, ever.
Yet He was executed as a criminal. Jesus prayed from the cross,
"Father, forgive them, for they don't know what they are doing"
(Luke 23:34 NLT). You may not be able to pray that prayer right
now, but consider where it leads us. It schools our hearts in empathy and "trains our spirits in compassion," as Eugene Peterson has
written. More than this, he continues, it allows "for the possibility that 'they know not what they do.'"[8] How many of our parents
intended the harm they caused? How many acted in ignorance
and are ignorant still? How many are stuck in their woundedness,
unable to see, to move?

This is what we're doing now. We are training our spirits in
compassion. When we do this, we discover or remember again the
frailty of our parents, the burdens they bore, the weight of their
own parents' sins upon them. And we'll find something much
larger happening. When we truly see others in all their humanness,
we become more alive, more awake, more fully human ourselves.

AFTERWORD . . . WITH DR. JILL

Our parents. We learn from their strengths and their shortcomings. None of us need perfect parenting. All we need, as stated by D. W. Winnicott, is "good-enough mothering."[9] However, as we have heard, many receive *not-good-enough* parenting. In normal development, when children are frustrated, they learn tolerance and the capacity for delayed gratification. Too much frustration, chaos, and unpredictability creates varying degrees of trauma and traumatic self-states. The greater the trauma, the greater the need a child has for survival mechanisms and the development of increased resourcefulness. The human spirit seems to compensate over the long haul. But what once protected the psyche can become maladaptive later on. We are all both victims and perpetrators of our human condition and thus our human frailty. When we can see ourselves in our humanness and then offer that same perspective to others, even our parents, we bear witness to each other's lives, to our stories, and to our places and purposes in history.

Our parents were once children living under their parents' roofs. Who were they as little people, and what were their hopes and dreams? Can we begin to see our parents as people, separate from us, in the context of their stories? After all, if they were not our parents, they would not have that powerful parental hold, bonded by our dependence upon them for our survival, and we might be able to see their personhood more clearly.

However, once our parents reached adulthood, regardless of their childhood experiences, they were responsible for dealing with their past hurt, so as to not inflict it upon us, the next generation. Therefore we, too, no matter how unfairly, are called into our own healing journey and are accountable for our own awareness.

This does not mean we should bypass our hurt or at *wrong*. Naming reality is not only important but a n in the forgiveness process. We can be full of feelings ab while at the same time giving up our fantasy of a just world. *Fake* forgiveness involves following the letter of the law, going through the motions from our heads, with no heart connection or change. Fake forgiveness is forcing the *should*s and *ought to*s of forgiveness by glossing over one's childhood too quickly. It's like saying, "They did the best they could," without acknowledging our parents' fallible humanness.

In spite of Leslie's father's lack of character and just plain lacking, God intervened and developed Leslie and her siblings to a place beyond their father's capacity. Their father did not deserve their love and attention—they deserved those things from him! But giving to him was a way of redeeming what the locusts had eaten. Not everyone should sell their house and move to be near an undeserving father or mother. Sometimes we move toward a parent in hopes of still getting from him or her what we longed for as a child. This deferred hope and wish can keep you from growing up on the inside. It may mean you are still wanting your parent's approval and looking for validation in your mom's or dad's eyes, to finally hear the words *I love you* or *You're a lovable daughter* or *You're a competent son.* But it is possible to forgive and love out of a place of mercy, not out of what your parent has "earned." When you've taken God in as the Father you never had, you can be generous out of the character He has developed in you.

One caution: moving toward a wayward parent when you are not in a place of emotional stability could be to your detriment if it is too emotionally disorganizing. For example, if you feel traumatized, dissociate, lose chunks of time, blur present and past realities, or are not able to generally function (work, get out of bed, take care of children), or if others observing you have concern for you, this can be evidence of a post-traumatic stress regression. These types of reactions warrant seeking help from a professional counselor, even if you have sought help in the past. At the very least, you must have a strong support system, which may include a support group where traumatic family issues are freely discussed. Check resources in your community or at your church for a solid recovery program or care ministry. Although not substitutes for professionally trained clinicians, many churches have lay counselors who are supervised by a licensed therapist and can help contain you in between therapy appointments as an added source of support.

Twelve-step groups that support the idea of seeking God or a higher power—something greater than yourself—such as Adult Children of Alcoholics/Dysfunctional Families (ACA), Al-Anon, Survivors of Incest Anonymous, or Co-Dependents Anonymous (CoDa) can be especially useful and understanding when you are struggling. Certainly, if being with a parent involves the risk of physical harm and ongoing abuse or throws you into a derailing crisis, you do not want to reenact your abuse and now make it your children's abuse as well. That does not represent a healthy moving forward in forgiveness and mercy.

In our and our parents' humanness, we must be witness bearers for each other. Given that we have the capacity to observe ourselves and others, and we can maintain ourselves as fully separate individuals, we can then allow ourselves to move toward our parents and to know more about them. Go to others who know your parents' story or parts of it, as Leslie did—those who can bear witness to who your parents were and their lives. If possible, seek out your parents' peer group, their siblings or friends who knew them when they were young or perhaps your age now. This can be of value to help you see them more objectively (noting that others have their own biases and hurts, but they could be different from yours).

When my grandfather was in the last days of his life (almost ninety-eight and still driving), he was asking to see his estranged son, the youngest of his four children—my father. Instead he got my brother and me and our kids, whom he'd not known. My grandfather and my father had had a falling-out a couple of years earlier, similar to what I'd had at twenty-five with my dad, and my brother earlier than that. It was my father's habit to cut those closest to him out of his life one by one until there was finally no one left who knew of his whereabouts. After my grandfather's funeral, I sat with my father's siblings—my aunt, his only sister; and my uncle, the oldest and last family member to have had contact with my once-gregarious dad. Unsolicited, both offered explanation and interpretations for his disappearance from all of our lives. One, he didn't want to be found; and two, perhaps his rage, bitterness, and paranoia had elevated to the point of mental illness. It was their explanation, but nonetheless, it helped me to have two people who grew up with him offer some attempt to make sense of what had troubled and puzzled us all. I found comfort in their willingness, having known me as a child, to acknowledge that things were not right in my world. They were my witness bearers.

We, too, may be called to be witness bearers someday in children's lives around us. I think of a family member by marriage who lived in our home for a couple years, and his two young sons (five and eight years old at the time), who would visit and play with my children as cousins. When these young boys' parents divorced, it was beyond two people going their separate ways and sharing two kids; it was a fight to the emotional death and the permanent removal of one parent from the children's lives and society at large. Someday I expect to see these boys as adults, when they want to know for themselves an expanded version of what happened between their father and mother and an additional explanation of why their father had been sent away. I will be waiting and willing with open arms to hear them and, as desired, to shed light on events and people that altered the course of their lives forever. This is the stuff soap operas are made of—but this is also real life, mine and yours.

Study Questions

1. Who are your parents? Describe your father or mother as if speaking to someone who doesn't know that person.
2. What do others say about your father or mother? Have you discovered ways in which your parents' peers might see them? In what ways do others' perspectives of your father or mother differ or echo your own experience?
3. If you were to observe your parents objectively, as individuals outside the role of parent, what strengths might you see in them? What are their limitations as people?
4. Who are you more like, your father or your mother? In what ways are you similar to or different from either parent?
5. What are one negative way and one positive way your father or mother made you feel about yourself? What are one negative

behavior and one positive behavior you adopted from your father or mother?

6. Have your parents ever let you know any of their hopes and dreams for life? Do you believe they've lived out any of those dreams? If yes, what? If not, what, as best as you can ascertain, got in the way of their hopes for life?

7. Who did your parents have to lean on, guide them, and care for them during their growing-up years?

8. Think about your parents' childhood experiences. Is there any part of their story you feel compassion for?

9. Do you think there is any connection between the ways in which your parents were wounded and what may have spilled over into the way you were raised?

10. Because we have a limited perspective on our parents' lives, it's often difficult for us to see them clearly. We need others to be our witnesses, to bear with us and reveal to us what they see from the outside looking in. Whom would you be willing to talk to in order to gain deeper understanding of your parent?

FOUR

The Unforgiven and the Unforgiving

The weak can never forgive. Forgiveness is the attribute of the strong.

—Mahatma Gandhi[1]

WHAT HAPPENS IF you don't stop and look on the other side of the road? What if you don't want to see the wounded lying there? What does that bypass look and feel like? We're going to follow others down their roads to see where they end up after walking past their beat-up parents, barely looking. Their stories may help us decide.

———

I'm in my kitchen, sitting at the table with a young man. He is holding our new puppy in his arms, a Yorkshire terrier, who is lying back, basking in his affection. William strokes her tenderly while telling me about his mother. I cannot miss the contrast: his tenderness with the dog compared to the portrait of his mother. She is a rageful woman, he tells me. She yelled at her sons continually when they were home. If they left their shoes at the door or they didn't wash the car well enough, she railed at them—"You don't appreciate me! You can't do anything right!" If someone spilled the tomato soup, she would scream. The brothers did not dare bring a friend home after school. One day they came home from high school to find a list of jobs tacked to the front door—a list that ran from the top of the door to the bottom. She was unpredictable, William tells me, her anger explosive and corrosive, usually containing insults and deprecations. As William speaks, I see the anger and hurt in his face come and go. But finally he shrugs when I ask him about forgiveness. His face stiffens.

"I know we're called to forgive. But I guess I never thought of forgiveness toward her. She is who she is, and I don't care. My father says she changed right after I was born. No one knows why or how she changed. I don't care how or why she is the way she is. I don't care about forgiving my mom. I just don't care. And that attitude might be no good, but that's where I am right now. I'm out of the house, married now. I hardly see her anymore. I'm never going to expect anything from her. It doesn't hurt anymore, so I don't need to forgive her. I'm just living in the here and now, and I just try and forget what happened in the past."

———

I find life experiences like this everywhere—people with good reasons for walking past a father or mother. I find stories online, from men and women angry at one or both parents. They detail their parents' crimes, which include all that we have come to expect: abandonment, abuse, silence, poverty. One man describes his father as a "wretch" who abandoned him as a child. When the father became ill later, he ended up in the hospital. The son refused to see him. When the father died, no one came to claim the body. The son felt no regrets for his actions. His father was "just another despicable, nasty old man," he wrote. A man to whom he owed nothing.

No one on this busy site wrote in to convince him otherwise.

While working on this chapter, I met my brother Todd for lunch at a popular restaurant in Anchorage. We cherish our relationship. We're close in age, just eighteen months apart. We weren't able to have friends over at our house after school, so we were each other's playmates, building forts together, playing football and baseball, and competing in pushups and pull-ups. We've both settled in Alaska. We each have six kids, and though we are a four-hundred-dollar plane flight away from one another, we share our lives as much as we can.

Over our fancy seafood chowder, we talked about our meals growing up. "Remember the chicken?" one of us began. Ah yes, the chicken that appeared once or twice a month, the only meal that tasted good! How we would all eat it down to the barest bones, then pull off the cartilage and suck out the marrow and eat the soft ends of the bones until almost nothing was left. We complained together about our kids, who waste half the meat when they eat chicken, and admitted that sometimes we gnaw what's left off of what they throw away.

Then we were on to the eggs. "How many did you eat a day?" I asked Todd. We could buy cracked eggs from a local egg farm for twenty-five cents a dozen. My mother bought maybe ten dozen a week. We ate egg sandwiches for lunch almost every day. We had eggs for supper some nights, and we ate eggs in between meals, since there was little else to eat. "Remember the egg foo yong we tried to make? Eggs with sprouted soybeans?" We grimaced involuntarily at the memory; then we laughed with the joy that comes from remembering something safely distant, and with the relief of being with someone who knows, who was there. Who else knows where we came from? But we stopped smiling.

"I went to bed hungry a lot," Todd told me.

I nodded. I was hungry too. We both stole candy bars from stores over the years to fill that hunger. This is just part of the story. We'd talk about our clothes another time. Homemade, worn-out hand-me-downs. Our one pair of shoes a year, which were chosen for us. Ugly, brown lace-up shoes that looked like boys' shoes— that we girls had to wear—eliciting mockery from our classmates year after year. My freshman year of high school, I stole cheap clothes from K-Mart stores when I could, desperate for invisibility, to hide my otherness. Then the threats from the electric company that the electricity would be turned off, the bank threatening to repossess our house—again and again. The shame of our poverty. Our stories all shaped by our father, who refused to get a job he could actually do, like maybe in a factory, work that didn't require much skill. We knew he couldn't do much, but he could have done *something* other than spend the little money we had driving around New England, not selling anything.

We'd been bitter, angry, resentful, and hateful. And we'd walked right past him, for decades, not seeing. Not caring to see.

I read another woman's story online. She is seeking forgiveness from her children for a serious and damaging lapse of judgment. Sexual abuse is part of the story; disbelief is part of the story. The abuse went on for a year before she ended the marriage with the abuser. Her children, all grown now, have cut off all communication with her. They will not allow her to see her grandchildren.

None of her children will listen to her or heed her plea for for-giveness. She feels hopeless, buried under a mountain of hate and unforgiveness. She doesn't know what to do, so she writes begging others for help.

This is the voice of the unforgiven. But her quest gains no sympathy—at least from one reader. A woman writes back to her, lashing out in unrestrained anger, furious that this woman has dared to post on a forgiveness site. Alluding to her own sexual abuse, she calls the mother "sick," and tells her that her children will never forgive her. Indeed, she insists they *should* never forgive her.

Often we think the cost of forgiving is too high. But we do not con-sider the cost of not forgiving. We do not see who we're becoming. We're so busy trying to extract our debt from our parents that we do not see what it has done to us.

A friend called me again about her father. I've heard many stories from her over the years. She is deeply angry with her father, though she left home ten years ago. When she's around him, she only wants to run away. He's the kind of man who enters a room and sucks all the air out, leaving people gasping, she's told me. "How do you grow up with a man like that, who has to control everything and everyone? If any little thing didn't go the way he wanted, including spilling your milk at dinner, he exploded—or sometimes he might laugh, but you never knew which it would be." I know how she coped. She and her brother learned to sit very quietly, to hide in their rooms, to avoid being noticed. She is still fearful of him and seldom returns to visit. Her anger spills over to her mother as well for not leaving him.

I heard a lot of pain and anger in her words, but the phone call was not really about her father. It was about her, the isolation she feels, her inability to make friends, how hard she works to keep her parents out of her life. Near the end of the call, her voice lowered and hardened: "I know they want to see my kids a lot more than they do, but they don't deserve it. And finally I have some power over them. I'm not proud of it, but I feel some satisfaction in causing them a little pain. It's their turn now."

To choose unforgiveness is often to choose a form of vengeance and punishment, large or small. We know a price should be paid. We feel as though we've already paid it. Now we want our parents to pay, certain that we're righting the cosmic scales of justice. There are so many ways to do it. Tell their secrets. Refuse to help. Simply disengage and withhold. Erode their reputations publicly. I've seen this as a writing teacher, in students who come into the classroom, leaning into their memoirs with such pointed vengeance, their words like swords, and the subjects are usually former spouses—and parents. I read it in published memoirs that slice and dice family members with ridicule and exposure. It can feel just, and even right, this kind of settling of accounts: *You failed to do this for me as a child; now I will fail to do this for you. Measure for measure. Isn't this biblical? "An eye for an eye"?*

Most of all, revenge is an attempt to ease our pain—and sometimes to make our marks in publishing. One woman published a book detailing ways to get even when "Mr. Right Turns Out to Be All Wrong."[2] *The Woman's Book of Revenge* released in 1998, to little acclaim (only five customer reviews on Amazon at this writing[3]), but her website lives on, dishing out inspiration for "your darkest revenge fantasies."[4]

I understand the temptation—we all do. And most of us try out the power of revenge at some point in our lives. Here's a revenge account from my own files. When I was in my early twenties, I lived on the same tiny island in Alaska as my brothers and parents-in-law. When I married at twenty, I joined a family who commercial salmon fished off a remote, forty-acre island near Kodiak Island. Everyone worked long, intense hours on the ocean in all kinds of weather. But the work was assuaged and fueled by lavish meals prepared by my mother-in-law, Wanda. For breakfast, she would often serve fried potatoes, homemade muffins, eggs, fruit, juice, and coffee. Her husband, DeWitt, my father-in-law, was usually on time for breakfast, but never any other meal. When called for lunch, which was a similarly bountiful spread, or the more simple suppers, he would take his time and finish whatever task he was doing. He was the patriarch of the family, with many wonderful qualities, but timeliness wasn't one of them. He knew we wouldn't start without him. When he was ready, he would amble up to the house, oblivious to the fact that he was keeping the rest of us waiting anywhere from ten to thirty minutes nearly every meal. The food would get cold; we'd all be watching our watches. But no one said anything—DeWitt ran on his own clock.

One morning DeWitt announced, with great flourish and drama, that he was making breakfast. This was a landmark event. Like many men of his generation, DeWitt didn't cook. I had not seen him so much as cut a carrot or wash a pan, so this was big news. Apparently he hadn't liked the fried potatoes that morning, so he was going to do it right. That next morning, DeWitt got up early and started making the fried potatoes, putting in lots of onion, just the way he liked it.

While he was cooking, making a great show of his efforts, I cooked up a plan of my own. Tired of his come-when-I-please approach to the meal table, I decided to give him a taste of his own tardiness. I made the rounds on the island to the rest of the family and gave the same message to each one: "When he calls you for breakfast, wait at least ten minutes before you go. Just wander in when you feel like it." They looked askance at me—this was clearly an act of insurrection, but they were annoyed also with his thoughtless habit and agreed.

At last the two massive skillets of fried potatoes were done. The call to come to breakfast was issued with great excitement and anticipation. But everyone was good to their word and didn't come right away. I sat in my kitchen in my own house, watching the minutes tick by, with anticipation of my own. Finally DeWitt would know how it felt. But every minute that passed felt heavier rather than lighter. Finally I could hold out no longer and left my house for theirs, walking the short distance between our house and their cabin briskly now. By the time I got there, a few others had just come. We were about ten minutes late. DeWitt was clearly frazzled and annoyed that we hadn't come just when he called. The meal was eaten with disappointment all around. The acclaim he had hoped for hadn't come. I ate a pile of guilt-fried potatoes, crisped up with vengeance, and it didn't taste very good. The aftertaste was worse—a distinct bitterness that wouldn't wash away with water, milk, or anything. And nothing changed. Meal times went on as before. The venture was a bust all the way around—except I knew I would never knowingly pursue vengeance again.

Unforgiveness takes us back to Jonah's terrain. Last we checked in, he wasn't on terra firma at all; he was stuck—a lump in the digestive tract of a massive fish. No matter how you view this story, as fanciful fable used as an extended metaphor or as fact, he's got something vital to show us.

During those three days and nights in the fish, Jonah, under-standably, had a change of heart. He called out to God, "Those who cling to worthless idols forfeit the grace that could be theirs. But I, with a song of thanksgiving, will sacrifice to you. What I have vowed I will make good. Salvation comes from the LORD" (Jonah 2:8–9). And promptly, the fish puked him out onto dry land.

Off he went to Nineveh, reluctantly obedient, to declare the message God had given him: "Forty more days and Nineveh will be overturned" (3:4). I don't imagine that he preached with vigor and conviction. Yet the worst possible thing happened. Everyone in the city believed his words, from the servant to the king on the throne. They repented, to a one, following the desperate decree written by the king: that everyone fast, put on sackcloth (the clothes of mourning), and "give up their evil ways" and "call urgently" on God. "Who knows?" the king wrote in the decree. "God may yet relent and with compassion turn from his fierce anger so that we will not perish" (3:3–9).

And that pagan king's hope came true. God, seeing their repentance, was filled with compassion for them and relented from his threat of destruction. Our man Jonah could not have been angrier. "I knew you'd do that!" he said to God. "Isn't that just what I said back home? That's why I ran away to Tarshish!" He went on: "I knew you are a gracious and compassionate God, slow to anger and abounding in love, a God who relents from sending calamity" (4:2). And can you hear him shouting this angrily at God: *"I knew you are a gracious and compassionate and loving God!"*? Yes, God's com-passion becomes a cause for rage when it's turned on your vilest enemies. And Jonah ended his diatribe like this: "Now, just take my life. It's better for me to die than to live . . ." (v. 3). I know how he mentally ended that sentence: . . . *in a world where my enemies get off scot-free.*

Can you hear it? *What are You doing, God? You can't run a world like this!* Of course, what Jonah had forgotten was that he himself had been the recipient of God's love and compassion. In fact, God had already rescued him twice in the last few days: from the near-sinking ship and from drowning. He'd also protected him as he wandered the streets of his enemies, preaching against them. What were the chances of emerging unscathed from that task? Jonah would gladly take it, all of God's compassion, toward *himself*—but there were limits, he thought. God's forbearance and forgiveness should only go to the good people, people like him. Jonah had forgotten his very own words, spoken in the fish, "Those who cling to worthless idols forfeit the grace that could be theirs" (2:8). The Ninevites were no longer clinging to their idols, but Jonah still would not share with them any of God's grace.

God did not keep silent. "Is it right for you to be angry?" God queried Jonah (4:4 NLT).

The story should be over here. Though we're not happy with Jonah's selfish pouting, the plot is resolved: Nineveh had repented and God had relented. There are enough twists and turns—not to mention a whale—in the storyline as it is. But there's yet one more turn of the plot, involving a plant and a worm.

After this last exchange with God, Jonah morosely hiked up to a promontory east of the city and set up camp. He had one tiny, fervent hope left—maybe God would relent *from relenting* and still destroy the city! He settled down to watch and hope. But the sun was unmercifully hot. God kindly grew a plant to give Jonah shade. Jonah was so happy about the plant giving him shelter. But the next day, God sent a worm to kill the plant. Now, unshaded, Jonah felt faint. It was the last straw for him. Not only were the people he despised still alive and—horrors!—humble and repentant, but now his beloved shade tree had died! The one thing he'd loved in that entire landscape, that shading plant, was dead, while the people he hated were alive and thriving. He was so angry at this injustice and unfairness that he wanted to die, and he told God so: "I'm so angry I wish I were dead."

> But the LORD said, "You have been concerned about this plant, though you did not tend it or make it grow. It sprang up overnight and died overnight. But Nineveh has more than a hundred and twenty thousand people who cannot tell their right hand from their left, and many cattle as well. Should I not be concerned about that great city?" (4:10–11).

That's the end of the book. God ended the whole fantastical, twisting story with that question. "Should I not be concerned . . . ?" Jonah had more concern for a vine than he did for the people of an entire city. He never saw them as fellow human beings, as deserving of pity. His heart was so hardened against them— women, boys, old men, little girls, grandmothers, fathers—that he never saw them as fellow recipients of the compassion he himself had received over and over. Jonah was so corroded and blinded by his anger that he couldn't countenance others receiving what he himself had received: grace in place of judgment. His fury was so great that he wanted out of the whole business. Not simply the business of being a prophet, but the business of being alive. He preferred death over living in a world where the wrong people are forgiven. Do you see him there, who he had become? A prophet of God, glowering under a plant, wishing 120,000 people dead. He was as trapped and imprisoned in his hate as when he was in the gut of the fish.

Jonah missed it all. He was given an extraordinary chance to see the heart of God, a God who offered life instead of death, a God who loved those who were His enemies, a God who would later come and say, "You have heard that it was said, 'An eye for an eye and a tooth for a tooth.' . . . But I say to you, love your enemies and pray for those who persecute you" (Matt. 5:38, 44 ESV). Jonah would not and could not see God's immense vision and desire for the people and even the animals of that city. He was stuck in a smaller world of his own making, where everyone got what they deserved—except him.

In his book *Free of Charge: Giving and Forgiving in a World Stripped of Grace*, Miroslav Volf warns us that "in trying to overcome evil by enforcing justice, there is always the danger that we may be 'overcome by evil' ourselves. . . . Revenge multiplies evil . . . and threatens the world with destruction."[5]

Clint Eastwood gave us such a world in his movie *Unforgiven*, winner of four Academy Awards, including Best Picture in 1992.[6] It's a western, set in the frontier town of Big Whiskey. The action begins in a brothel when an angry customer slashes the face of a prostitute, Delilah, unleashing a tide of events. Her face and her livelihood are now ruined, but the lawman in that frontier town, played by Gene Hackman, declares that a payment of horses will cover the crime. The four women of the brothel, outraged by this insult and injustice, pool their money and offer a thousand-dollar reward to anyone who will kill the wrongdoer, Davey. From one act of cruelty, we descend into a world powered by revenge, where rigorous accounts are kept. Delilah is out of a trade. The brothel keeper is out the money he'll lose from her services. The sheriff, Little Bill Daggett, has a score from the past with William Munny, Eastwood's character, who goes after Davey for the reward. Everyone has a debt to settle. Everyone's keeping score, made all the more obvious by the entrance of a tagalong biographer, who carries a notepad with him and jots down every event, who killed whom, when, where, and how. It's never clear whose account of the past is more reliable, but it matters little. Every party knows only one way to make it right: killing the one who owes him or her. As vengeance plays out, the humanness of each character recedes as the body counts rise. There is no sense of innocence or loss here. The night after Davey is killed, Strawberry Alice, the one who initiated the reward, yells out: "He had it coming! They all have it coming!" Munny's sidekick, the Schofield Kid, who kills Davey, nervously justifies his first murder by saying, "Well, I guess he had it coming." Munny mumbles back, "We all have it comin'."

Ned, Munny's only friend, is killed in retribution by Daggett's men, his body set in an upright coffin to incite Munny further. It does. Munny blasts into town, heads for the saloon, and blows away the brothel owner to get to Daggett. The two men shoot up the room, randomly killing bystanders. As Daggett finally lies dying, with Munny over him, ready to finish him, Daggett growls, "I don't deserve this, to die like this . . . See you in hell, William Munny." "Yeah," Munny growls back.

As the movie closes, we know we've been there already, a place where everyone keeps records of wrong, however inaccurate and untrustworthy. A place where every action is paid back, not measure for measure, not eye for eye and tooth for tooth, but a leg for an eye, a life for a tooth. Everyone pays; no one can forgive; no one is forgiven. Everyone alike is under the sentence of guilt and death, and no one is able to escape.

Unforgiven is not just a movie. A few years ago, after speaking at a women's retreat, an older woman came up to me with tears in her eyes. "I don't want to forgive my father. He abused me during my childhood. I'm still angry. I don't want to forgive." She looked at me with both defiance and pleading in her eyes. Then she added, "What should I do?" I looked at her closely. She had lived her whole life with this anger. She was probably seventy-five.

We can choose to remain in this world . . .

"I'm so angry I wish I were dead."

"You don't deserve to be forgiven."

"I don't care about forgiving my mom."

"My father was just another dirty, nasty old man."

"He had it coming! They all had it coming!"

. . . Or we can choose to break free.

AFTERWORD . . . WITH DR. JILL

They don't deserve my forgiveness, I can't—I won't . . . I don't want to forgive!

Holding on to unforgiveness is sometimes our only connection to a person. And we feel that the only way God and others will see that individual's wrongs is through our pain, that our protest is the only accounting/accountability that exists. As if even a traumatic connection sewn together with the threads of unforgiveness is better than nothing at all. Keeping an account of others' wrongs assures us of our right to anger, bitterness, resentment, and revenge.

The anticipation of vengeance, the replaying of revenge fantasy daydreams over and over again, and the middle-of-the-night, anxiety-ridden anger are born out of a need to effect some impact or change. When acted upon, they either fall flat, make us feel ridiculous, or in worst-case scenarios, end up with some legitimate victims serving jail time when their revenge schemes end badly. Unfortunately, injustice is not a respecter of persons, nor are the human emotions that are evoked.

We *do* have a right to be angry. In fact, we must get angry in order to propel ourselves further down the road to forgiveness. Getting in touch with our anger empowers us to move out of a childlike, victim mode and enables us to tolerate looking at reality. Anger is the comma in our sentence, where we pause, but not the period at the end, where we stop. To be energized out of denial, fantasy, depression, and victimhood is essential. However, at a certain point we will max out the benefits of our season of righteous anger. At that point of maximum productive benefit, if we continue to protest without surrender, the probability becomes greater that we will become another variation of what we abhor.

While anger has a place in healing, it is the bitterness, resentment, and revenge of long-term unforgiveness that becomes problematic. The difference between emotional health and emotional illness, sane and insane, is often determined not by what one thinks or feels but by what one acts upon. When we want vengeance, it is so hard to wait on God to take action, especially when we see the wicked prospering (see Psalm 37:7), and to have compassion for our enemies—may it never be! Who, then, will see what they have done? Who will know our hurt? Why don't we get to have our justice?

My friend and fellow psychologist cohost Dr. Dave Stoop is a longtime expert and writer on the topic of forgiveness. In his book *Forgiving the Unforgivable,* he emphasizes that "forgiveness always involves the moral side of life." When someone has wronged us, we are torn between our values of justice and fairness, of right and wrong, and "another part of us that holds on to feelings of love for that person, compassion for their predicament, and a desire to show mercy."[7] To move toward one side of this dilemma makes us feel as if we've abandoned the other side, yet neither pole feels satisfying in and of itself. It's that age-old tension where two seemingly opposing values must coexist side by side.

Jonah struggled with this same moral tension. As we do as well. Is our hate like Jonah's? If those who have wronged us are forgiven too soon, when do they suffer, as we have at their hands? We want to be vindicated. We want everyone to know. We find ourselves screaming from the rooftops in so many ways. How did our parents not see, not know? Why did they not fix themselves before they had us? Many of us believe in God and His word, some of us are leaders at church, and most of us consider ourselves caring and loving toward others, so forgiveness should come more easily to us.

But sometimes our hurt has been too direct and too severe. Just the thought of our perpetrators may bring a visceral response to our bodies and minds. The hate that rises from our pain can feel positive—it can feel like power. But it is the wrong kind of power. It creates a false sense of protection, like pulling a gun on an unexpected intruder. We think we're saved by our weapons, but so often the guns are turned on us and we are the ones who are shot.

According to the theory of attribution, we are all masters at maximizing others' wrong behavior and attributing malicious intent to even their neutral actions when we feel hurt and violated. In contrast, we tend to minimize the impact or significance of our own "accidental" wrong behavior and justify it with our believed noble intentions, whether they materialize or not. This contrast is reflective of our inability to fully integrate good and bad in ourselves and others—a developmental milestone on our journey to maturity. When you've been the recipient of a lot of "bad" from another person, the gulf between any "good" in that individual seems wide and deep, with no bridge in sight. We are all Jonahs who, in our unforgiveness, question whether we can or want to do the work of building that bridge of forgiveness that gives us the grace to see both good and bad in the one who has wronged us.

Study Questions

1. Who are the Ninevites in your world, the worst of the worst in your life—the "wicked" people who have hurt you and those you love, the ones you see prospering while your life suffers from their destruction?

2. What does Jonah's "shade-giving plant" represent in your life?

3. Who or what is the "worm" that deprives you of what little good you may feel you have and deserve? How are you continuing to victimize yourself rather than claim your power back?

4. How do you express your justifiable feelings? Would those closest to you in your life now consider you an angry, resentful, or unforgiving person? If yes, why? If no, how would they describe your expression of anger, resentment, or bitterness, even if it is rarely seen?

5. Pray about your attitudes as you overlay Jonah's life picture and worldview onto your own picture. Do you see any of Jonah's attitudes in yourself? If so, how? Take a moment to put it into words.

6. What do you gain by holding on to your unforgiveness?

7. What do you lose by holding on to your anger, bitterness, or resentment? Can you identify any benefits to releasing your unforgiveness?

8. Read Psalm 139:19–24 and reread Matthew 5:43–48. How do these verses validate your emotions toward hurtful people? What do these passages say about what to do with the strong feelings toward those who have done you wrong?

9. Have you been able to release any anger, bitterness, and resentment from someone who has harmed you? If so, how? What ideas do you have about some healthier ways to work through your strong feelings?

10. What role does pride play in relation to your hurt? Is there any part of you that desires to continue in relationship with the person you are not forgiving?

The Heart of Forgiveness

To be a Christian means to forgive the inexcusable, because God has forgiven the inexcusable in you.

—C. S. Lewis[1]

AT 3:00 P.M., the ice cream parlor at the rehab center opened up. It was the "ice cream social" hour, as announced on posters around the campus. My father knew about this, of course, since ice cream was one of the great pleasures of his life. I wheeled him into a cheerful room with curled wrought iron parlor chairs and tables with red gingham vinyl tablecloths. A large woman in blue scrubs stood bored behind the counter, waiting to serve. One woman was there, a youngish woman with Down syndrome, lavishing great attention upon her bowl of ice cream. She did not look up as we entered. A mother and daughter talked loudly at a table in the corner. Despite the disguise, I soon discovered the ice cream parlor was in cahoots with the rest of the institution. They knew Howard Leyland was allowed only one scoop of sugar-free vanilla ice cream and two tablespoons of sugar-free chocolate syrup. I smiled outwardly as I took the Styrofoam cup and ordered a second one just like that for myself.

We ate, the two of us, at our table together. We ate the same ice cream, the same syrup, in the same kind of cup. My father and I. We did not speak. I ate as slowly and deliberately as he did.

We were nearly done when a tall man I hadn't seen behind us wheeled to the front counter.

"I want some more ice cream."

"I'm sorry, Mr. Johnson, but you can't have any more."

"I just had one scoop. I want some more ice cream!" His voice rose. I could not see his face, only his bald head and his neck, now reddening above his shirt collar.

"No, I'm sorry. You can't have any more. It's all gone. The parlor is closed now." The woman was calm but resolute.

"I want more ice cream!" he yelled now, pounding his fist on his chair.

"It's all gone, Mr. Johnson. You can't have any more." She had clearly faced this insurrection before and spoke in a monotone meant to sound comforting yet firm.

Furious, he tried to stand, pushing his weight up on spindly arms while still yelling. "I want more ice cream!" he persisted, swearing this time.

The woman watched sadly, shaking her head, as the man finally gave up, dropped back into his seat, fuming and cursing, and inched his way out of the parlor.

My father and I watched together in silence. An inmate tries to break out. Out of his wheelchair, out of his body, out of the jail where a grown man who has run his own life for sixty-five years can't get one more scoop of ice cream, not by yelling or threats, not for anything. My father is right. This is the house of horrors, where you go when you not only lose part of your brain function and therefore part of your body's function, but what little is left that you can do, you are not allowed to do. Such helplessness. So much is lost as we age; so much is stolen from us. Only a few are angry, it seems. Perhaps we should all be angry. I think of Dylan Thomas's famous poem, "Do Not Go Gentle into That Good Night" and the line "Rage, rage against the dying of the light."[2] If we are lucky, we live long enough to earn infirmity. As we journey toward infirmity, we lose so much along the way: friends, jobs, a child, maybe a marriage. Many lose and even forget their dreams of a good life that never materialized.

But a catalog of all we lose is not the whole story.

I looked at my father sitting just two feet from me. He was not looking at me; he was eating his ice cream as if I weren't there. I didn't know what his fears were, if he was living them out at that very moment: being stuck in a rehab facility where he knew no one, and if he was lucky enough to graduate, he'd return to a room in a nursing home. Who dreams of ending their days in a nursing home? But he was not alone anymore. His children had found him.

For me, halfway through my life, I was realizing more and more that the story of my life was not written by the man across from me. My story had been written by another. It was because of that story that I'd decided to come, after all. The ones I know who have moved deeply into forgiveness know this story too. It is the tenderest and truest I know. You may already know it. It's time to tell it again.[3]

———

A father had two sons, who worked with him in a family business. The business was prosperous enough to support servants as well. It was a good life for all, but the younger son tired of living under his father's rules in his father's house. He wanted out. Of everything. Out of the business, out of the family, and out from under his father's authority. He wanted to try out life in that faraway city he had heard so much about, where he could do whatever he wanted. It was months before he dared, but finally, with courage in hand, he approached his father:

"Dad, I know you're going to give me my inheritance when you die. But I want it now. Why should I wait to enjoy what is rightfully mine? I need that money now, while I am young enough to use it."

The father understood the meaning of this request. He knew that his youngest son considered him as good as dead. He knew, too, that the money would be wasted. The father was shaken with shock and sadness but granted his son's request and let him go. The son was gone the next day.

After such an affront, a violation of all manners and even laws, most fathers, perhaps all fathers, would have festered in their fury against such a son. After all he had been given! An entire life receiving generosity and meaningful work, a home, security, loving parents. He lacked nothing. Not even freedom. He'd only had to ask, and freedoms were granted. Any normal father would wipe his hands of such a son, send him out with a boot and a curse, remove him from his will entirely. But not this father. He let his son go with full provisions, with all he had been saving for his son's future, all he would need. It was in his hands now, his son, his beautiful son. He remembered the day he was born. He thought of their meals around the table, stories told at night to wide, listening eyes. The favorite supper he would request on his birthday. . . .

He tried to keep his business going, but his son's absence haunted him through his days. Hours every day he watched the road over the mountain, piercing every figure and group that wandered past, looking for the familiar gait, the particular way he swung his arms, his oversized feet.

The son, however, did not give a thought to his father. He ran toward every fancy he had imagined in the prison of his father's house: loud parties, the finest liqueurs and spices, expensive imported clothing, horses, gambling, prostitutes. But it was not long before his money was gone—all of it. Without money he lost everything, even food for his table.

Famine hit the entire land as well. The young man could find no work but slopping pigs. He fed the pigs, but no one gave him even a morsel of food. He was utterly lost, invisible, indentured to men who cared nothing about him.

Hungry and destitute, he remembered his father's home, and how well his father treated even his hired hands. Even his servants had full meals!

Why had he ever left? He'd thought his father was cruel and restrictive, but now he saw how different he was from his boss at the pig farm and how different from the partyers who cared only for his money. He was generous to all, even the servants. And especially to his sons!

But the wayward boy had no right to call himself a son anymore. In demanding his inheritance, he had given up his rights as a son. He had one hope left: maybe his father would take him back as a servant. He knew that was all he deserved.

Meanwhile, the father could not stand the distance of that far horizon. He found himself on the road one day, almost unintentionally, but there he was, his own feet moving in relief toward that far country in which his son was living. It made no sense to leave his business, but he couldn't stop himself. He was behaving as no father would, humbling himself this way, hoping it was not too late, hoping the son was still somehow alive, body and soul. That the thieves and betrayers and cities of men and women who cared nothing for his son had not consumed him in his naïveté.

One day, some distance down the road, he saw a figure. He peered, made out the outline of his frame . . . Did he dare hope?

It was him!

The father did not walk with dignity; he charged toward his son, arms already out, calling. When he finally reached him, before the son could say a single word—that he was sorry, that he regretted his scandalous behavior—the father's arms were around him.

The son received the hug, overwhelmed by his father's exuberance, but he knew he must speak the words his feet had trudged out the long way back.

"Dad, I've done wrong. I've totally screwed up. Against you and against God. I've ruined my life. I'm not good enough to be your son anymore. But please, treat me at least like one of your servants."

He had never spoken truer, more sincere words. But the father was not interested in payback. He saw the depth of the boy's repentance. And when they arrived at home, instead of granting his son's reasonable request to become a hired hand, the father shouted to the servants, "Quick! Bring the best robe I've got, and put it on my son! Put my special ring on his finger and sandals on his feet. Bring the fattened calf and kill it. We're going to have a feast! This son of mine was dead, but is alive again; he was lost, but now he is found."

Who is this father? He's not like any father I know. That's because this father is God Himself. This is the kind of God we have, a Father running to welcome his errant son or daughter home, forgiven. I've walked that same road home. It was my own homecoming that enabled me to come after my father, to sit with him as he ate ice cream in rehab.

———

It's such an ecstatic scene, the story I just told, and we'd like to leave it there. But the story goes on for a few more paragraphs.

The man's other son, the older son, who had remained with him through the years, wouldn't go to the party his father was throwing for his runaway sibling. He was angry both at his father, for forgiving and reinstating his brother, and at his wastrel younger brother. Such undeserved mercy! Here he had remained in the harness, but no one was throwing a party for him. What an unjust, ungrateful father! Like Jonah, the older son could not endure the mercy shown to someone else—blind to all that he himself had received.

The father came to him and reminded him who he was and what he'd already been given: "Son," he said, "you are always with me, and everything I have is yours!"

———

Isn't this really about us? It is. It *is* about us, and it is about God the Father. No matter how dressed up or down we've lived, whether we were the ones who ran away or the ones who stayed, resentful, we've all rebelled against our Father's house in one way or another.

I am certain the father in our story forgave the elder son as well. But this is us, most of us, who in varying degrees insist on taking what we think is ours and going off to a far country—to Alaska, to the room next door, where we want to make and run our own lives, without parent or authority. "Each of us has turned to his own way" (Isa. 53:6).

This is the truth about us. We all need forgiveness for the way we have fled our Father. For all the ways we have used and misused one another. Eugene Peterson describes sin this way:

> Sin is anti-gift and anti-personal. Sin ruptures or sabotages living relationship. Instead of receiving we take. We decide we don't like the bread given to us on our plate, throw it on the floor, and grab the bowl of ice cream from our sister. The world of grace, which requires personal, open willingness to humbly ask and gratefully receive, is set aside for a depersonalized world of manipulation, violence, efficiency, control. . . . We do it a lot. And so we need forgiveness.[4]

We extract what we want from one another, and even more from God. Yet we keep on taking, until we take His place entirely in our own lives. Isn't this what most of us want—to be the god of ourselves? Even when our own self-rule leads to ruin and despair, we may still hold the course. But the Father absorbs the cost of our rebellion and comes after us. He longs for us. He pursues us, and while we are yet a long way off, turning toward home, our Father sees us and, swelled with compassion, runs to us and throws His arms around us.

With His arm on our shoulders, we confess the truth about ourselves and the truth about Him. He listens, calls us son and daughter; we were dead and now we are alive. He gives us the keys to the mansion—and the party begins.

This is who we are. We are a found, forgiven, celebrated people. This is not about our mothers or fathers right now. This is about us. What's been done for us. Who we really are. The God of Everything has come after us—and whether we're still in that far country or we've turned back, there is only one true home, one real freedom: in our Father's house. Whether we've been in His forgiving embrace yet or not, it is there waiting for us. Where will we find the strength, the courage, to forgive? It is here. We can forgive others because we are forgiven. Of everything.

———

I sat over my bowl, stealing glances at my father. I longed for him to know this. I longed for him to see beyond the confines of this ice cream parlor, with its forced cheeriness, beyond the limits of his body, his age, and even his own past. He didn't know that it was because of this story that I came. That without divine interruptions in my life, I would be going my own merry way, a way that would have steered me clear of this man. This is the man who, after finding out I had had another child, had written a letter advising my husband to get a vasectomy. *Six kids is too many,* he'd said. As the father of six, I suppose he knew what he was talking about, but it was hardly a comforting thought. I wanted to tell him that forgiveness is a real force at work, not just in me, but all around the world, changing people and villages and families and entire nations. That its power has been brought into the worst wastelands of evil—onto the battlefields of genocide in Rwanda, Sierra Leone, and South Africa. This is so because forgiveness is not simply a private affair between us and our welcoming Father. There is a necessary out-wardness to forgiveness that has long been at work in the world.

We hear of it when Peter, the disciple, asks Jesus the question any one of us would have asked, fearful of the outrageous gener-osity of forgiveness. What if someone comes to you over and over, asking to be forgiven for the same old sin, the same old crime, all in one day? "How many times do I forgive him?" Peter wanted to know. "Seven?" An incredibly generous and even frightening amount! Clearly, a little forgiveness is a dangerous thing! But Jesus' answer takes away all accounting: "Not seven times, but seventy-seven" (Matt. 18:22). Meaning, no counting.

How can this be? When Jesus saw Peter's face and the expres-sions of the others around him who had just heard His answer, He told another story to explain:

> A king decided one day to settle his accounts with his ser-vants. One servant, somehow, owed him millions of dollars. He couldn't pay, of course. It was an unpayable amount. The king, concerned about upholding justice and the laws of the land, ordered that the servant and his wife and children and all that he owned be sold to begin to pay back the debt (all common practice in that culture). But the servant, about to lose every-thing, fell on his knees and begged for another chance. "Have patience with me, and I'll pay you everything!"
>
> The king was moved by his tears and desperation and for-gave the debt, wiping it out entirely, and then let him go free.
>
> The squandering servant walked out from the king's pres-ence as though he had never taken an illegal dime of his money. A multimillion-dollar debt—erased. (Matt. 18:23–27, author's paraphrase)

Just as in the first story, here it is again. Our accounts, the debts we've racked up against a holy God, are cleared. So what did this man do next? What do *you* do when you have passed from death to life, when you've been pulled through the jaws of death not by your own effort but by the very one you've wronged? And emerging now to not just freedom, but to a whole new start, as if you'd never gambled, never extorted money from your boss, as if you've always done right and good and nothing else?

What *did* he do? Did he run home exuberantly to prepare a gift for this merciful king? Did he gather his family and friends and ask them for forgiveness, too, to begin a whole new life? Did he turn toward those who owed him money and erase their debts, as his had been forgiven? None of the above.

Running out from the king's presence, he tracked down another servant who owed him a pittance, and started choking him. "Pay me what you owe me!" he snarled in the poor man's face. This man did exactly what the other man had done just hours before with the king. He fell on his knees, terrified, and begged for mercy, with the exact words the other man himself had used before the king. But the forgiven servant was flinty, unmoved. He ignored the pleas of his fellow servant and threw him in prison until the debt was paid.

Who, after being forgiven of such an immense debt, could not forgive someone else's small debt against them? It is absurd, pathetic, and mean. And yet, isn't this what I have done? I am set free, yet I run, crying, "You owe me!" to my father and to many others, to people who are themselves entirely bankrupt. What do I think I will gain by this?

The king found out what happened, and when he did, he called the first servant back—and he didn't mince words. "You wicked servant!" he said. "I forgave you all that debt because you pleaded with me. And should not you have had mercy on your fellow servant, as I had mercy on you?" (Matt. 18:32–33 ESV). Then, in anger, the king threw him in jail until he could pay all his debt.

As Jesus concluded this story, He told his disciples, "So also my heavenly Father will do to every one of you, if you do not forgive your brother from your heart" (v. 35 ESV).

The warning is real. The king treated the first servant as he had treated others and tossed him into prison. There he would live out the reality of the prayer, "Forgive us our debts as we forgive our debtors."

What is the true measure and scope of the offenses we are asked to forgive? The Scriptures above say they are nothing compared to our own offenses against God. I believe this is true, but I confess that it rankles. It's not an easy truth for sons and daughters who have suffered under their parents' rule. Aren't we better than our harsh, abusive, negligent mothers or fathers? I can't pretend there is not a huge qualitative difference between how I have lived my life and how my father has lived his. But I have to let go of this. Who gave me the cosmic measuring stick that knows all hearts and judges rightly? Clearly, we are equal to our parents in this: we are all masters of self-defense and self-deception, with little apprehension of our offenses against a holy God.

And I realize something else. It is not really justice that I'm after. Most of us think we want justice and equity as a means of balancing the universal scales of good and bad. But I have come to see we mostly want relief. The measures we devise on our own to bring us relief often have little to do with fairness and real justice.

The cosmic scales of justice that we appeal to are not what we think. Our own debts are paid for. Our parents' debts are paid for. This is far better than justice—this is mercy. But we have to know, as beautiful and hopeful as this story is, the cancellation of our debts is not entirely free. Other accounts tell us the real cost of the father running down a dusty roadway, arms out, the real cost of a king saying, "You can go home free." This is a transaction far beyond a pencil crossing out a million-dollar debt, far beyond the wave of a king's scepter. It would take much more than this. It would take two trees, a hammer, iron spikes, torn flesh, the body, blood, and life of God's own Son. It would take and cost that much.

That's the ancient claim of Christianity. No other faith makes that claim—that everything you've done wrong can be utterly covered and forgiven by another, by God Himself. Simply for the sincere asking. It cannot be earned by your own kind intentions and good works. The "good work" has already been done on the cross. No matter who we are, we all believe at least in this: when wrong is done, a price must be paid. For millennia, tribal and indigenous peoples in nearly every country have enacted blood sacrifices—animal and human—to cover for sins. The idea will not go away.

In the movie *Flatliners* we see it again. Kiefer Sutherland plays a medical student, Nelson, who figures out how to return to the past. He and his fellow med students take turns going under a drug that causes them to die, to flatline, for a few minutes before they are brought back to life. While under the drug, hearts stopped, they are released into their childhood memories, but not the idyllic ones— the most traumatic immediately steal center stage. For Nelson, he is relentlessly pursued by a ferocious eight-year-old boy, Billy, who beats him bloody with whatever implement is available. Over time, we discover the backstory. The boy had been just as relentlessly bullied by Nelson when they were children. One rainy night, the gang of persecutors chased Billy up a tree, where he cried for mercy from the boys circling below the tree. Nelson threw rocks at him until Billy lost his grip and fell, screaming, to his death.

Nelson cannot shake either Billy, who returns to the present to terrorize him, or his own guilt at causing his death. He knows he deserves to die himself. So he puts himself under one last time. He climbs the tree in the rain and cries out, fearful from its height and what he knows he must do. And he does it. In the dark night, in the wind, anguished and terrified, he leaps from the high branches, falling to his death. It is only this death-sacrifice that finally frees him from his guilt and from Billy's avenging spirit.[5]

Just before He died, Jesus uttered three words that made the purpose of His life and then His death clear: "It is finished!" (John 19:30). The word He chose for "finish" was a Greek word used in accounting. When written across a bill, it meant "paid in full." That was for us, for every one of us who claims it. Our debt, our massive, impossible, unpayable debt against a holy God is covered. We walk away cleared of our debts. Free.

We leave this horrific crucifixion scene unburdened, fully alive. But what was all this for? Was it for you alone, to secure your precious happiness and freedom? What was all that for? The coming of God-in-the-flesh, His arrest, the beatings, the cat-o'-nine-tails, Jesus' flesh shredded; the earthquake and darkness, the temple tearing in two; then three days later, His return to life? Was His pursuit of you through the long years of your life—was it all really just to secure your Get Out of Jail Free card? To give you a happier life?

Yes. And no. The God of Everything has more in mind than you, as important as you are. And more in mind than the unburdening of your soul, more in mind even than you forgiving your father and mother.

This is costly forgiveness that sets us free indeed—but the freedom you've been given is not really yours. It does come with strings. We all are born into this world with strings attached: we are made by a Creator, born from a mother and father; we often enter the lives of siblings and grandparents. We enter a world filled with people bearing alike the stamp of God-madeness. We are attached to all of them. When God freed us from our debts against Him, He freed us not to live however we choose, not to pursue our own whims and fancies—but to love more fully. We owe each other honor and kindness. We owe our very lives to our Creator and Redeemer. We owe Him and one another sincere love. We owe our mothers, our fathers, our wives, our children, our husbands, our neighbors, the stranger—we owe them all, yes, forgiveness.

If you have prayed the Lord's Prayer ever, even once, you have already prayed for this very thing. "And forgive us our debts, as we forgive our debtors," we say with folded hands and bowed heads, usually in church. There it is again, "debts," what we charge and cost one another. But do you hear those words? How many years did I say them before I really heard them? What have we asked God for? We should be terrified, because in truth, we probably didn't really mean it. Do we really want to ask God to apportion his forgiveness of our daily sins according to our forgiveness of others' sins against us? Jesus must have known the fear and offense in these words; they're the only words of the prayer He explicated immediately after speaking the Lord's Prayer. As soon as He ended, He immediately explained: "For if you forgive men when they sin against you, your heavenly Father will also forgive you. But if you do not forgive men their sins, your Father will not forgive your sins" (Matt. 6:14–15).

The meaning is clear. When we are forgiven by God, we

become a forgiving people. The correlation between the two is so necessary that the Scriptures speak it both ways. Here, God's daily forgiveness of our sins will be measured by our own forgiveness of others' sins. Elsewhere, repeatedly, we are urged, "Just as the Lord has forgiven you, so you must also forgive" (Col. 3:13 HCSB). There is no simpler way to say this. We have been forgiven so that we may forgive others and live out the reckless, perfect compassion of a God whose love for the world and for us knows no bounds.

How far does this forgiveness extend? You may be stuck at the starting point, thinking you are beyond forgiveness yourself. I don't know what you've done, but I know what Peter did, the disciple who loved Jesus most passionately. He dropped everything to follow this man—his vocation, his friends, his family. After three years of witnessing the most astounding healings and teachings, after declaring his undying commitment and love for the man he had come to believe was the Son of God, after vowing to follow Him to the death, Peter abandoned Jesus the very night he was needed most. Terrified for his own safety, that night he refused any knowledge of the One he loved and trusted more than anyone else. He said, "I don't know that man" not once, but three times, the last time in the hearing of Jesus Himself, who looked straight into his eyes while being led away to die. But we know the story doesn't end there. After His resurrection, Jesus returned, and for as many times as Peter denied Him, offered forgiveness.

We've all denied Jesus. We've all turned away from Him at key moments and in trivial moments. We've turned away from one another. We are all guilty. But if the one with the greatest responsibility and knowledge can commit the worst sin and be forgiven, so can you. Don't be stopped by your own failings and sin.

What of those who have suffered the most horrific offenses:

murder, rape, destitution? Does it still hold up? Must we still forgive? The 2008 documentary film *As We Forgive* follows the path of three people in Rwanda ten years after the 1994 genocide. One man killed another with a machete in the maelstrom of the Hutu-Tutsi annihilation. Ten years later, he is in the presence of the murdered man's daughter, unable to look at her, consumed by shame and guilt. His only desire is to be forgiven by her. She has lost most of her family in the killings and has little desire to forgive this man. She didn't even want to see his face, but over a period of months, through the encouragement of a Rwandan mediator, she agreed to see him.

The camera does not lie. When they meet, her face is troubled; she is angry, deeply unnerved by his presence, which painfully resurrects all the murdered members of her family. She cannot forgive. We understand. Over weeks and months, she continues to meet with a mediator.

In the end, the camera catches her bright face as she joins a group of men and women and children carrying bricks to build a new home for another victim of the genocide. Through months of talking, praying, she is forgiving the man who killed her father. She is beginning to smile again.[6]

We are a found, forgiven, and celebrated people that we may live out another kind of life, a Godward life of mercy toward all, a life of feeding others. After Jesus forgave Peter, He gave him a job to do: "Feed my sheep" (John 21:17). Peter's forgiveness came with a call to action.

I am the first to confess I have ignored this far too long, this uncomfortable fact that God has somehow mysteriously linked the measure of His forgiveness with my own forgiveness and blessing of others. I have nurtured my own hurts and meted out my judgments for so long—to many more than just my father. It is terrifying to realize how much I have missed all these years, how little of God I have apprehended, how narrow I have made His mercies.

What does it mean, then, to forgive our parents? It means we let them go; we erase the debts they owe us. We wipe out their accounts. Our parents may owe us a lot. We know what we needed from them: nurture, food, security, education, love, blessing. Many of us got less than we wanted and needed. And still do. How long shall we keep that account running?

We shall begin to let it go. To release our fathers, our mothers, from our own judgment, from an accounting that holds them hostage, and us as well. They will still face God's judgment. We cannot alter that. It does not mean they are off the hook from all accountability, especially if they have broken the law. There may be issues of justice to be settled, even for the protection of potential future victims. Even when legalities are pursued, forgiveness can still be given.

Who has done this? I know many. Here is Michelle, whose father used to punch her in the face and knock her to the ground when she came home late at night:

> When I decided to go on this journey, I said, "I'm going all the way through forgiveness. I'm not going to stop halfway and blame my father for my troubles." I wanted to reach a place of total forgiveness. I didn't have the tools to do that until I met Christ. I didn't have peace. I didn't have grace. I didn't have mercy. Once I had those myself, I could finish that journey. A lot of people stay in that halfway place because they can still blame that person. They make a career out of it. I decided to go as far as I could.

———

After my father and I finished our ice cream, we wheeled slowly into the end of a hallway for a good-bye. I found a plastic chair to sit in.

I had a small Bible with me. It was my mother-in-law's. I held the maroon leather book in my hands, filled with memories and sadness, filled with last days, knowing how soon the end can come. Wanda, my mother-in-law, had died in a house fire out at our fish camp three years before. In the Alaskan wilderness, with no fire-fighting resources, the house burned to the ground in the middle of the night. Several people broke into the fire-consumed house, trying to rescue her, but no one could get to her in time. She went to bed that night and fell asleep not knowing it was her last night. The fire likely broke out from the stove; the smoke filled her room, and without waking, she was gone. She was a woman who loved God, who gave to others her whole life, one of the most selfless women I had ever known. A woman very different from my father.

My visit that day was not an easy one. My father couldn't speak. I couldn't take him outside the rehab center for a drive. We had been stuck inside, going nowhere, for the last three days. *Now, how do I leave?* I wondered.

"Is it okay to read just a few passages from the Bible, Dad?" I asked. I didn't want to offend or take advantage, especially in his current state.

He nodded at me, looking straight into my eyes. I was startled both by his nod and his full gaze. He was like a child before me at that moment. I felt deeply responsible for him.

My father loved books, and I think he loved words. Though

he never spoke much, he used to read the newspaper aloud to us whenever he could. I opened Wanda's Bible, turned to Isaiah, to the beautiful words of invitation, and slowly read, "Seek the LORD while he may be found; call on him while he is near. Let the wicked forsake his way . . . Let him turn to the LORD, and he will have mercy on him, and to our God, for he will freely pardon" (55:6–7).

I glanced up. My father was listening. He was still attentive to me. When did this ever happen? It was a God-made moment.

"We are all wicked, compared to the Lord, Dad," I explained. "I am as well. But He *will* freely pardon us!"

He reached for a yellow legal pad beside him, placed it on his lap, and painfully wrote four words. He handed the pad to me.

I like your viewpoint.

I was amazed and looked at him with wide eyes. "Do you know that He loves you?"

He had a slight frown and almost imperceptively shook his head. I knew he was a reader of Richard Dawkins and had read atheist literature for many years.

"What is holding you back, Dad?"

He took the legal pad back and slowly, with difficulty, wrote one word. He handed it to me.

He had written the word *trust*.

I nodded. "Yes, trust. That's a big word. That's really important. Can I write you some more about this when I get home?"

He took the pad back and labored over it, writing with a crabbed right hand. I was surprised to see it was cursive writing, and he had written the words, *I look forward to your words of wisdom.*

I blinked at sudden tears. I had never seen him so soft, so open to me, so open to what I love most.

"I love you, Dad. I hope to see you again. I'll write you as soon as I get home."

———

Mercy. I *did* love mercy. Everything I did for him on that trip, he had never done for me as a child, as an adult. As anything. But that harsh accountant's voice in my head began to quiet. The bile of injustice began to calm. I knew who I was. I was no longer a child. I was no longer trapped in my own resentments. I was no longer a debtor to God. I had been freed myself, and now I wanted him to know that freedom as well. I thought of one of my favorite lines from Psalm 119: "I run in the path of your commands, for you have set my heart free" (v. 32).

———

What will this look like in your life? What has it looked like in other's lives? I will illuminate myriad ways and times and places where forgiveness has been offered, where it has awakened the living dead, where it has enlivened the dying, where it has been offered—and refused. There are surprises ahead for all of us.

AFTERWORD . . . WITH DR. JILL

At what age do we stop expecting our parents to pay? At forty? At fifty? At sixty? When do we look at adulthood for what it is—not a fulfillment of all our childhood hopes and dreams but a sobering, mature reality that *all* of us are broken and fall short of the glory of God? Our purpose is to do the good we can, with what we are given, to bring forth beauty from ashes and to become more Christlike—not necessarily *because of* our parents but *in spite* of them. We must do the work of forgiveness to create something different, something better, to pass on to our children and grandchildren. After all, we are writing our future generation's history as we live it today.

As we journey forward, we also reflect. We remember our history not to revere it but to know ourselves and others in context, to better learn and grow from our and others' mistakes. We are to work through our heartaches, devastations, and struggles in life, but we're not to make idols of them. Lot's wife looked back longingly at the sin of Sodom and Gomorrah (Gen. 19:26). We can stubbornly cling to our pain and refuse to live beyond it, but God is greater than the power of our past.

How do we shift our hearts? How does the nice idea of forgiveness, or the unthinkable request from God to forgive for real, move us from head knowledge to a sincere process of the heart? Let us look at where we've been and where we are going as we read further.

We have looked at Jonah's running, resistance, and closed heart. We realize that in order to forgive we must turn from our own ways that probably aren't working so well. We must face what we fear, what we know to be true. Using our adult eyes, we must look back to our childhood memories and remember those difficult events. Remembering makes us wise and teaches us discernment. But as we begin to face our stories, our fears, our memories, we need help. It's too much to bear alone. Who in our life is safe now? Is there someone with whom we feel loved and cared for or perhaps a trained professional who will keep our confidence as a place to start our unpacking?

With that person, confess your memories out loud. Sharing and crying with another is much more effective in moving us toward healing than all the crying done alone in our rooms. You must remember the child you once were, to give that child the validation and voice she or he never had. Talk therapy brings healing and has a positive impact on our brain chemistry. Being heard decreases our overwhelming fear that our problems are too much. When we feel some containment and know we are no longer alone, our sense of hope increases. We then have greater emotional room internally to consider other aspects to our story.

We can then sit with the thought of our parents' humanity. Allowing our own humanity to humble us softens our hearts and enables us to begin to see those who have hurt us with compassion. We can consider the impact of their upbringing and the children they were. This is not to ignore or condone what they are responsible for; it is to broaden our perspective to include understanding.

As we do this, we must remember the biblical principle of Matthew 7:1–2, that "you will be treated as you treat others. The standard you use in judging is the standard by which you will be judged" (NLT). God holds us to the same standards we hold for others. This should elicit a measure of fear and humility, and realization of our shared need for grace.

We have been forgiven much ourselves; we have much to forgive. With heavy and grateful hearts we move along in our process of forgiveness. We see how far God was willing to go for us! The pain we have borne from others does not exonerate our own sin and shortcomings before God. If we need forgiveness, how can we not give it to our parents?

Even with newly open, contrite hearts, we may still find obstacles ahead. Our parent or parents may be unrepentant and may continue their hurtful ways toward us. Can we still forgive them? Most secular sources insist that forgiveness is a two-person process requiring repentance from the one who has wronged us. It is certainly much easier to muster up compassion and to let go of hurt and anger when we are vindicated by the other person's remorse. The tragedy in this view, though, is that when there is no remorse or ownership of wrongdoing by the other person, we are left hopelessly bound to him or her, thus enabling the person to continue to hurt us. Why would we continue to seek after those who hurt us as our only path to comfort and freedom? Yet we do. But God's way is much better! When we forgive we take the person off of our hook and put them on God's hook.

> Do not repay anyone evil for evil. Be careful to do what is right in the eyes of everyone. If it is possible, as far as it depends on you, live at peace with everyone. Do not take revenge, my dear friends, but leave room for God's wrath, for it is written: "It is mine to avenge; I will repay," says the Lord. On the contrary: "If your enemy is hungry, feed him; if he is thirsty, give him something to drink. In doing this, you will heap burning coals on his head." (Rom. 12:17–20)

We can only do our part in forgiving, as much as we can, "as far as it depends on us." We cannot free our parents from their parts; we can only set them free from us and in turn gain our freedom from their emotional hold on us.

Though we describe a process here, and this book follows a certain chronology, it's important to know there is no prescribed exact order to our healing. Forgiveness often does not follow a nice, predictable path lifting us out of our pain. It can be messy at times, as we circle round and round our same issues. It can take time, depending on the depth of what must be forgiven. Remember that our feelings, all of them, are part of our process and that anger and protest are part of our healing too.

But God understands our limitations and knows we can't simply power through the forgiveness journey. We must be sincere. God lovingly shows us that our ongoing anger distorts our view of life and humanity. We are to allow our feelings and struggle with our protest but resolve to be willing to surrender our fight.

Study Questions

1. At this point in your forgiveness journey, how is your heart feeling? Is it heavy or hopeful? Still reluctant? Take a moment to pray about any resistance or closed heartedness to forgiveness you are feeling.

2. We are called to love because Christ first loved us. Does it not follow that we ought also forgive to the depth we have been forgiven? Have you connected with your own vulnerable need for forgiveness?

3. What specifically have you gone to the Lord with in order to receive forgiveness? Are there personal transgressions for which you still need to seek His forgiveness?

4. What repetitions do you see from one generation to the next (generational strongholds) that you need to name and confess, claiming authority in the name of Jesus Christ?

5. Christ's forgiveness is a gift to us. How is His command to us to forgive also a tremendous gift to you personally?

6. You know how difficult forgiveness can be with a chronically hurtful parent. The forgiveness journey most often involves repeated processing as hurt is compounded. Christ tells us to forgive those who sin against us seventy times seven (Matt. 18:21–22). Who benefits from this supernatural kind of forgiveness?

7. What if your parent does not acknowledge his or her wrongs? The world tells us to forgive only those who express genuine sorrow for their wrongs against us. What's the downside to this condition of forgiveness? What does the Bible tell us about this?

8. What are some ways to forgive if your father or mother does not seek your forgiveness? How do you humble yourself, give up your pride, and still forgive? What role do boundaries play?

9. Anger is a true emotion, but how it is expressed can be productive or harmful to both people. Can you make a decision not to act on your bitterness or resentment as you work through it? How does the idea of mercy and the element of choice factor in to help your heart to shift? Are you willing to take ownership of your feelings and be responsible for them?

10. Have you seen forgiveness walked out in someone else's life? Have you ever experienced the blessing of a repaired

relationship by offering undeserved forgiveness with no expectations? Or have you offered forgiveness and the relationship did not repair?

The Prodigal Father and Mother: Honoring the Dishonorable

For judgment is without mercy to one who has shown no mercy.
Mercy triumphs over judgment.

—James 2:13 esv

In an early scene of the 2012 movie *Being Flynn,* a mother and her twelve-year-old son, Nick, are sitting in a parked car facing a bus stop.[1] We hear the narrator, a man, speak:

"All my life my father has been manifest as an absence . . . not a presence, a name without a body."

The camera closes in through the front windshield of a car, where the woman and boy sit.

The mother, played by Julianne Moore, looks weary. "If he doesn't show up this time, I'm going to kill him," she says with tired but fierce conviction.

"Can we get ice cream if he doesn't show up?" the boy asks. His freckled face is intent upon the bus stop, but he's already made other plans.

"There's the bus! There he is!" the mother says hopefully as a silver city bus lumbers into view and noisily brakes. The doors *shoosh* open. Someone steps down. As the bus pulls away, they lean forward.

"No, that's not him," the mother announces flatly. The bus grumbles off down the street. "What kind of ice cream do you want?"

"Chocolate."

They drive away.

The father, Jonathan, does write letters, though. By the time Nick is grown, he has a collection of maybe a hundred of them, which he keeps and has read again and again. But the father doesn't show up until Nick is twenty-eight.

Being Flynn is based on Nick Flynn's memoir of his father's return to his life and the troubled relationship that ensued. In many ways, the story is familiar. We can't help but hear and see in its unfolding scenes a kind of replay of the prodigal son story. With one major revision: here, as in so many households, it is not the rebellious youth who runs off after his own starry dreams, but the father who deserts his child. What could be more unnatural, more upside down, than this: the ones who bring us into the world abandoning us to the world?

Here is the story of one of my father's departures. I was twelve. We had a little money left in the bank from the sale of our last house, three years before, that we had been living on. Fewer than a thousand dollars were left in the account. Since my father did not work, could not get a job, we lived on our ever-dwindling bank account, wringing food out of a stone most of the time. Our cupboards had always been sparse, but now we were down to less than thirty dollars a week for food for seven of us. We were eating canned mackerel for dinner, boiled chicken necks, or cracked eggs that we bought for twenty-five cents a dozen. It was either fall or winter. We kept the thermostat at 62 and layered on old sweaters to stay warm. My mother was valiantly going to school, enrolled in a six-month training program so she could get a job afterward.

On one of those days, with my mother in classes and the six of us in school, my father went to the bank, withdrew all but a few dollars to fix his car, and then motored off to another town. He planned to be gone forever.

We found him one night at a motel a month or two later, all of us in the car. He came back, promising that he would get a job and keep it. By then we had no need of the other things he was supposed to do: Be a husband to his wife. Show interest in his children. I never wondered then why he did not do any of these things. I hadn't been around other families to know what fathers did. We had other, more important needs: a roof over our heads that the bank wouldn't repossess; lights and electricity on—no more threats to turn them off. Food on the table, gas to get to school. When he returned, we had no fatted calf to slay for him, no ring for his finger—just a ring for his nose, I think he felt. There was no celebration that he had returned for us either. We knew he came back under compulsion only.

I know many parents who left their families and never turned back—except maybe to send an occasional card. Rhoda's father, who abandoned her when she was a baby, randomly sent her a birthday card last year after years of silence. The card was cheap. "I think he picked it up at a gas station," Rhoda told me with disgust. Below the ridiculously sentimental message, he simply signed his first name. And one more detail: he spelled his daughter's name wrong on the envelope.

Stephen's father abandoned him and his mother when Stephen was an infant. Sarah's father left before she was even born. Caleb's mother took off when he was twelve, moving cross-country and taking his sisters with her, with no plans of ever coming back. Keven's mother, an unmarried schoolteacher, farmed him out to relatives at first, then foster families. She had no interest in raising her only child.

And there were other means of abandonment: parents who treated their children badly, who were dishonorable and left the kids to hold it all together at home the best they could. Darlene's parents were home most of the time, but they were so wrecked with alcoholism, mental illness, and adultery that she ended up virtually raising her two younger siblings.

The question is, what do we do now? We've confessed these sins against us. We've looked at our parents' own lives, trying to understand the hurt and harm that came to them. We've considered the price of not forgiving. We've gone on to read about the king who forgave the enormous debt of his prodigal employee; about the father welcoming his prodigal son home and honoring him with privilege he had not earned. We may even know our own debts against God are forgiven. How do we take the next step?

As we move toward forgiveness, maybe mostly by faith right now, help comes from a surprising place, from where we may least expect it. Help comes from the top of a mountain on fire, from the very finger of God, from stone tablets many think were given to bind us and weigh us down.

The Ten Commandments teach us how to live well and rightly with God and our neighbor, yet they feel impossible to keep. Who has not violated at least half of these commands? "You shall have no other gods before me. You shall not make for yourself an image . . . You shall not bow down to them or worship them . . . You shall not misuse the name of the LORD your God . . . Remember the Sabbath day by keeping it holy" (Ex. 20:3–8).

Then here it is, the fifth command: "Honor your father and your mother, so that you may live long in the land that the LORD your God is giving you" (v. 12).

At first we squirm and rebel at this fifth command. Forgiveness is not enough, then? We are given this added burden also, to honor our mothers and fathers, even those who are patently dishonorable? Or even crazy? This is Nick's revelation and painful conflict throughout the movie and memoir mentioned earlier.

At twenty-eight, in the midst of his own dead-end life, his cell phone rings. "Nicholas, this is your father. Could you come over here and help me move my stuff?"

Nick is disbelieving at first that the voice is indeed his father's, but he's eventually convinced. He goes reluctantly to meet him and to help him move out of his apartment.

"A pleasure to see you, Nicholas, under the circumstances," a disheveled Robert DeNiro says casually, as if greeting his son after a brief absence instead of almost twenty years.

Nick takes in his father's dissolute appearance, his bluster, his unearned familiarity, with a mix of shock and revulsion. It is not long into their first moments together that the father launches into violent rants against his landlord, against blacks and gays, balanced by equal rants about his own genius as a writer.

When Nick finishes moving his father, he shakily returns to his own apartment with this summation: "Here's what I found about my father: He's a racist, a homophobe, and he's crazy."

This is only the beginning of Flynn's story of his relationship with his father. We know what follows will be complicated and sad, and it is, but I watched the movie hoping for hope—and it comes. The two, father and son, improbably end up face-to-face again at the homeless shelter where Nick works and where the father comes, finally, to take refuge when his downward spiral ends any other options. Nick cannot figure out what to do with his father, who is indeed delusional, as well as obnoxious and offensive to nearly everyone in the shelter. But Nick, against all odds and his own demons, comes to live out the fifth commandment and tries to help him, repeatedly rescuing him from freezing to death while living on the wintery streets. In the end, Nick does all he can to keep his father off the streets and out of the homeless shelter, settling him in a small, safe apartment.

Neither father nor son makes any reference to faith in either the book or the movie, but the welfare of both father and son feels directly, if mysteriously, connected, much like the fifth commandment. The command to honor our parents is unique this way, set apart from the other nine by offering a promise that no other commandment offers: "so that you may live long in the land that the LORD your God is giving you." Both the injunction and the promise are important enough to be repeated in the New Testament. Saint Paul gave the command to us again, expanding the promise and the blessing even further: "'Honor your mother and father'— which is the first commandment with a promise—'so that it may go well with you and that you may enjoy long life on the earth'" (Eph. 6:2–3 NIV).

That it may go well with us. Yes, we want it to go well with us, even with prodigal parents and a lousy childhood. As impossible at it may sound right now, here is a way forward to a better life, a better future: honor.

I have found people who have done this, who have honored

parents who were not honorable. Who have stood on the hill, watching their father's or mother's disappearing back, and gone after them, pursuing them with honor they did not earn. These are people I know, real flesh-and-blood people whose lives I have watched for decades, who have lived what they tell me.

Jimmy, one of the kindest men I know, shared with me the story of his life with his father. His dad was a harsh, unhappy man. Outside the family people saw him as generous, but in the family, he was someone else. When Jimmy or one of his five younger siblings messed up, the child didn't get the belt but the fist—smacked and thrown to the ground, with bruises to show for it later.

One day, when Jimmy was young, while riding in the car with him, his father asked him to open the window. It was an old truck, and it took some muscle to crank it open. Jimmy couldn't. His dad beat his leg mercilessly.

Jimmy grew up fearful of his Chinese father, whose expectations of his oldest son were almost more than he could bear. Nothing Jimmy ever did was right. When he graduated from high school with honors, Jimmy's dad didn't believe it. "That must have been a mistake," was his only response at graduation.

Jimmy's father was an atheist and railed at God and the church so often that Jimmy, ironically, became convinced that God was real and gave his life to Him at fifteen.

Years later, Jimmy brought his fiancée, Joy, to a family dinner and excitedly announced their engagement to everyone. Jimmy's dad sat in stoic silence, angry that his son hadn't consulted him first. He refused to attend his eldest's wedding, and even forbade his wife to attend. For two years he kept a stubborn silence whenever Jimmy came to visit his mother. And Jimmy refused to address a man who would not acknowledge him.

Twelve years after Jimmy and Joy were married, with very little contact between them and Jimmy's parents, his mom and dad announced they were coming to visit them at Cape Cod. Their visit ended up being a turning point in their relationship.

Jimmy told me,

> He was the prodigal father to me. When they came to Cape Cod, every time I saw him, I wanted to love him. I wanted to have a relationship with him—we didn't have one at all. As soon as they stepped toward us that way, by wanting to visit, we moved toward them. We tried to show them that there's another way to live. Joy showed it to me. She was the antithesis of everything I had grown up with. We were very generous with them. They were always so focused on money, on keeping accurate accounts of who owed what to whom.
>
> We wanted them to know the Lord, and to see that we had found a different way. That the way we grew up wasn't the right way. We knew that we had been forgiven, and I wanted them to know they could be as well.

The four started playing cards at night and having fun together. Jimmy and Joy loved his parents just as they were. Incredibly, they became friends. The short visit lengthened to six months. The parents didn't want to leave.

Not long after, Jimmy's father had a stroke, and very quickly father and son switched roles. Jimmy became his parents' adviser.

> Even with all that I went through with my father as a kid, I still hungered for him and desired a relationship. But I was able through God's love to ignore the other stuff. There was plenty

of bad stuff, but it was taken away by the love and desire I had for my dad. I thought of him as the prodigal father, and me as the son who says, "I don't care what you've done; I'm so glad to have you back!" He still never told me he loved me through his whole life, but I knew he did. In his later days I would tell him that: "I love you, Dad."

His father walked toward him, turned toward him. And Jimmy and his wife cared for him in his declining years, attending to him after his stroke, and were present with him during his death. But despite all that healing, his father never asked for forgiveness. Neither did he return those needed words, "I love you, son."

What makes this a happy story? Jimmy and Joy could not change all of the outcome, but they honored an offensive father and forged a relationship of love out of a relationship of abuse and hurt. They themselves were healed by extending honor and love, even when neither was returned. This is the world upside down, or rather a world turned right side up.

Jimmy and Joy almost make it look easy, but I know that in the midst of it, it's hard. We don't want to be the ones who turn the world right side up! There's so much to protest. Why do we have to stand on the hill in the place of the father? That's where our own fathers should stand! That's where God stands! Why are we asked to give honor to those who do not honor us or others? Why are we chosen to take their place when all through our childhoods, and even now as adults, we needed the very same from them? Who put us here? It is unfair, yes. But we've already lamented that. We're moving beyond injustice and loss. We're moving on toward a life that is larger. Albert Camus wrote, "There is merely bad luck in not being loved; there is tragedy in not loving. All of us, today, are dying of this tragedy."[2]

We needn't die of this tragedy. We *can* do this. Most of us know instinctively that we owe our parents some kind of honor, simply because they are the ones who gave us life. Most of them fed and clothed and tried to raise us as well. Most of them love us, however incompletely. Those who are parents now hope their children will give them some kind of honor as they get older. Even if we are unsure about the existence of a good God, we understand the importance of honoring our elders.

Regardless of our faith commitments, its importance goes even beyond these recognitions. At the root of it all, we're called to respect our parents not because of their character but because of their position. Somehow, for reasons we'll never fully know, God chose *them*, those very particular women, those very particular men, to give us life. I smile ruefully at the irony many of us experience: God chooses for our parents men or women—or both—who do not know Him, who will not acknowledge Him. Or, if they do serve God, they are still terrible, harsh parents. It's a wonder we all survive! It's a miracle any of us come to faith. But we do. God is never limited by the limits of our parents and our homes.

But even when our parents don't feel worthy of our honor and respect, *God is* worthy of our honor and respect. And He's tied the two together: Himself as the sovereign Creator God, and our parents as our divinely chosen human creators. So when we honor our parents, we honor God. When Moses repeated these words from God again, later, we can't miss the connection: "Be holy because I, the LORD your God, am holy. Each of you must respect his mother and father . . . I am the LORD your God" (Lev. 19:2–3).

Even when a father tears his own family apart, we are enjoined to treat that parent not on the basis of his sin but on the basis of his God-given place in our lives. How does this bless us? How will "things go well with us" when we do this? We get a small taste of a perfect world when we extend grace and goodness to our renegade parents, reminding us of what is coming: a new world where all divisions are restored, all wounds are healed. The kingdom of God comes among us.

The good news is that we needn't wait for a warm, overflowing heart full of happy feelings to begin. The command does not require a certain set of emotions; neither does it command us to love our parents, or trust our parents, or obey our parents (though children are commanded to do this elsewhere). We're required to give them honor. Honor is a mandate, not a feeling, rooted in action toward the good of the other.

There's no single way to do this. But for all of us, it can begin with an honest accounting of our part in the troubled relationship. Our own guilt may be large or small, but we will need to take stock of it nonetheless. As noted theologian J. I. Packer has written, we are all, every one of us, "sick and damaged, scarred and sore, lame and lopsided, to a far, far greater extent than we realize."[3]

Last summer, I ran into a man visiting Alaska. We ended up sharing our stories. Larry told me about his mother and the unlikely events that happened some twenty years ago. His mom had raised him by herself after kicking out her alcoholic husband. In her ongoing anger, she physically abused Larry throughout his childhood, leaving scars and burns on his body.

Larry grew up and became a pastor, living in various cities around the world. One year, he began to prepare a series of messages on forgiveness. He was troubled as he studied and wrote his notes, preparing to lead others toward forgiveness, and he knew, finally, what he needed to do. He picked up the phone and called his mother. As soon as he dialed her number, though, his heart raced; he couldn't breathe. He slammed the phone down. When he was finally able to call again, she answered, and he began.

"Mom, I've been thinking about you, and I realized I've been harboring anger and bitter feelings toward you all these years. I'm so sorry. Would you forgive me?"

She was startled and stuttered for a moment before she responded. "Ahhh, well, that's fine. We all make mistakes." Uncomfortable, she wanted to end the call. Larry knew she was blowing him off. So he pressed her, and described his genuine desire to be forgiven of his anger and bitterness toward her. She finally answered, quietly, "Yes, Larry, I forgive you."

The next week, Larry's mother went to church for the first time, beginning a process of humbling and reconciliation between them.

Honoring takes many forms, as varied as personalities, needs, and circumstances. Dena began to honor her parents by going into therapy and facing the realities of her family dynamics, working her way back toward more honest relationships.

Keven honored his mother by writing letters to her, calling, flying cross-country twice a year to visit her care facility for years, though most of the time she did not know him. She had refused a relationship with her only child all his life. She abandoned him, but he did not abandon her.

Stephen honored his father, a man he had never met, by meeting him for lunch in another city, upon his father's request.

Yvonne honored her parents, both mentally ill, by maintaining relationships through phone calls and sending presents when visits weren't possible.

My brother Clark honored our father by caring for him in his last year of life.

Genevieve honored her parents-in-law by listening to them and eventually following their advice to leave a cultish, abusive church.

What has come of all of this honoring of less-than-honorable fathers and mothers?

Dena's family has opened up in new ways. The secrets and hardships of the past have been acknowledged and confessed. New memories are being built around a new sense of trust.

Stephen is not sure he'll see his father again. Sitting across the table from him, he stifled feelings of revulsion. His father looked far older than his sixty-some years. He was overweight, unkempt, and a smoker. Steve felt no desire to see him again.

Keven tells me the end of his mother's story. "My major wound was trying to figure out why my mom didn't care about me. Why she didn't show love, even in her later years." He accepted that she'd had psychological issues that prevented her from mothering him. But he still believed in the commandment to honor his mother, despite the fact that she hadn't honored him, and to forgive her.

My brother Clark had a tumultuous year in Florida, but he was able to help our father in many tangible ways: taking him shopping, providing company, bringing gifts, moving him from the nursing home to the rehab center and back. He felt a deep satisfaction and a sense of healing in serving his dad. Giving love and respect felt very close to receiving it.

For many adult children, honoring can take bolder forms—such as resistance and refusal to continue destructive patterns or wrong decisions. Randi honored her father by resisting his pressure to move back home after finishing college. He had controlled her all her life and couldn't let her out of his grasp, though she was twenty-three. So she rented her own apartment in another city. The distance between Randi and her parents allowed both sides to consider the hurtful ways they related to one another. Her father, accustomed to ruling with his steely will, was humbled by his daughter's new strength—and by a first look into his own heart. A new relationship began. He even began going to counseling.

Mary has reconciled with her controlling mother and honors her by maintaining a relationship with her, but she won't allow her mother to lure her back under her thumb.

When Wendy, twenty-four, told her parents she was planning to marry her boyfriend, they objected. Yes, he shared their daughter's faith and was of good character, but he was biracial. Wendy was deeply hurt by her parents' response but felt she needed to honor them. They were, after all, her parents. She broke off the engagement.

Eight months later, she realized her mistake. She was twenty-five and no longer under her parents' roof, and she recognized that their judgment had been unbiblical. Wendy married the man she loved the next year.

Since then, both parents have faced their own prejudice and have come to love their son-in-law. When he was diagnosed with cancer in the first year of marriage, Wendy's mother and father were constantly present with care and support.

Here is the truth. Honoring our parents can be messy and uncomfortable. We may not always know how to do it. Know that the other in your life—the mother or father, the spouse, whoever is in your life that strains forgiveness and mercy—will press you, will test you. That person may rack up continued debts against you. At the same time, he or she may want to return to a life and relationship that is no longer possible.

Debbie has reconciled with her once-distant father, and she works at honoring him, but he wants more. He wants to be her daddy again, for her to be his little girl. He wants to make up for his absences when she was a child. "It's too late for that," Debbie told me. "I'm forty-two. I can't give that to him now. That's over."

Your parent's life may be a mess, and you are just one of many whom he or she continually hurts and betrays. But in turning toward your mom or dad, in honoring that dishonorable parent, *you* are becoming another kind of person—a person of honor. And you are making it possible for your parent to become a person of honor as well.

When we dare to open our arms, large or small, when we dare to take a first step, it *will* go well for us in the land, because we have not allowed our parents or our own fears to kill what we cannot live well without: hope, faith, and love. But we must be clear: our hope, faith, and love must be placed not in our parents but in God.

Those who have hurt us may not repent—ever. They may not change in any way. They may continue to be hateful and hurtful. We still may not be able to trust them. Deanna couldn't allow her father near her children because of his anger, even after she had forgiven him. Joan has resumed a civil relationship with her controlling, vindictive father, and occasionally stops in to visit, but she maintains reasonable boundaries to keep him from taking over her life again. You may need to establish limits even in the process of forgiveness—of welcoming a prodigal parent home—but nothing need stop you from living out the command God has given for the good of the whole human family: "Honor your father and mother."

In the story of my own turn back to my prodigal father, I looked for ways to show him honor. I began to look beyond my own needs to ask larger questions. Why had he run from us in so many ways? And even when we gathered in occasional family reunions, he chose the empty room far from the rest of us. Something happened very quietly one day that began to bring answers.

Sometime between my visits, I was seized with the possibility of mental illness in my father. I had known since I was a child that he was not like others, but no one in my family knew anything about mental health. I had heard a whisper somewhere about my father going to a clinic to be observed and diagnosed years ago, but I knew nothing further. Finally, after one of my visits, I began an intensive online search.

I began with a guess, searching for information on schizophrenia. I read page after page, scrolling through every personality abnormality, until I found it described in detail on several mental health sites.

I stared with incredulity as my father's every trait was described, from the flatness of his emotions and his inability to form relationships with anyone, including his children, to his consistent choice of isolation rather than company. As I continued to search, I found yet more key attributes that described my father with uncanny accuracy: his placidness, his fixation on UFOs, and his anxiety about his own safety (but no one else's).

I stared at the pages for a long time. Why did I wait so long to find this: *schizoid personality disorder*?

I had one last question. I returned to the little white box on the screen and added one more word: *treatment*. My face blanched, waiting for the first entry to open. Then I read a second, and a third. They all verified the truth: there was nothing *I* could have done. Most SPD sufferers never seek treatment, and without it, there can be no improvement. Even with treatment, improvement appeared tenuous. But knowing this would have helped. I cried that day and the day after.

I sorted through the limited memories I had of my father, trying to parse out the facts: What was the disorder and what was him? And were they two separate things, or were Howard Leyland and his disordered personality all one and the same? It was a tangle . . . but relief came as well. It explained so much. It eased the questions of why he could not seem to love us. It explained why he did not seem to need us or anyone else. It was not our fault. We had not caused his detachment and disinterest or his harm. But I was still confused.

How much was he responsible for, then? If he was ill but didn't know it himself, could I truly fault him for his damage to our family, for his refusal to help us, for his abuse of my sister? Did the illness excuse these things? If he did know something from the whispered visit to the psychologist and didn't pursue treatment, then that made him more responsible, didn't it? But there was no money or opportunity for treatment. I alternated between relief, blame, and paralysis until landing on relief. It is always better to know, even when we can't discern the limits of disease and responsibility.

And though I felt certainty about this diagnosis and some relief, my conclusions are not the same as my siblings'. We have all tried to understand who our father was and why he lived as he did. Others have posited a difficult childhood, emotional abuse, autism . . . How can we know for sure? But for some, certainty and a sense of closure does come with a diagnosis.

A friend, Marie, tells me her mother was finally diagnosed with bipolar disorder in a care facility. Her mother was ninety. Marie struggled with her mother's bizarre and destructive behaviors her entire life. The diagnosis could not change the past, but it did change how she thought about the past.

Darlene's father, too, was diagnosed with a mental illness. As was Gayle's. Many in these pages discovered along the way that their parents suffer from depression, from paranoia, from bipolar disorder, from schizophrenia.

We'll likely never be able to dissect the distinctions between the illnesses and our parents' true identities. We'll never truly understand our mothers or fathers, whether they're healthy or ill, but full understanding is not a prerequisite to respect. The fifth commandment still stands. I do not see a codicil that releases me from it. Others, however, do.

A woman wrote online about her dilemma with her mother, a dilemma many adult children face. Her mom could no longer take care of herself, but none of her children wanted to take her into their homes. She was hateful, the daughter reported. No one wanted her presence in their homes. What should she do? she queried.

A few responded to her anguished question. One admitted that we all feel some kind of bond to others in our family, but dismissed it as simply biology and genetics. Morality had nothing to do with it. The most important thing, she wrote, is that you feel positive about yourself and positive about the way you treat other people. So do whatever will make you feel good.

Another advised her to give up on directives from a book of "fairy tales." Some parents don't deserve to be honored. Her mother clearly didn't deserve her attention and sacrifice. Put her in a nursing home and don't bat an eye, she directed.

Who *does* deserve our honor and our sacrifice? Only those who have sacrificed and cared for us? We will be small-hearted people, then, paying back only measure for measure, merely dispensing a calculated debt. The repayment of debts may fulfill a sense of duty, but there is often little joy, and seldom grace.

———

In March, my siblings and I flew down to Florida to see our father. It was the first time we had all been together in sixteen years. We rented a house near his nursing home for four days. On the next-to-last day, we picked him up at the front door, guided him slowly to the car, eased him into the front seat, collapsed his walker, and stashed it in the trunk. Then we drove him to our rented house, a clean, new home with a swimming pool, for the afternoon. We were tender and solicitous.

As he inched his way through the door with his walker, all of us hovering, trying to help, he glanced up from his painful steps at the modern, clean décor and quipped, "The lifestyles of the rich and famous." We all laughed, surprised at his acuity.

We led our father into a house that was not ours, but it felt like ours. It felt like home. We were together under one roof for the first time since we all left our childhood houses decades ago. We had gathered from around the country to welcome our father to our home, to bring him into our forgiveness. We did not require of him what he could not provide—an accounting of who he was, how he had treated us all his life. I did not ask him if he was indeed schizoid, if that whispered visit to a psychologist so many years ago had yielded the same report. We were the ones with the food in the cupboard, with the house to share, with a love that multiplied between us as we gathered to honor a dishonorable man who had chosen to live most of his life alone. We welcomed him among us, offered the best chair we had, the best food we had bought. We put a robe on his lap. We made a party for a man who hardly laughs, who did not show love for us, our love spilling over, multiplying in the rooms and at the table, like loaves and fishes.

In the midst of that afternoon with our father, I remembered these words: "You have heard that it was said, 'Love your neighbor and hate your enemy.' But I tell you, love your enemies and pray for those who persecute you." And next comes the reason for doing it: "that you may be children of your Father in heaven" (Matt. 5:43–45).

We are not God, nor shall we ever be, but in these small ways that feel enormous for us, we can be *like* God. And like God, we can give so much joy in welcoming a prodigal mother or father who doesn't even know how much he or she needs it. I wonder, whose joy was the greatest in the parable: that of the one limping home, repentant, in wonder at the party thrown in his honor, or that of the one who welcomed and forgave with embracing arms? I did not see happiness on my father's face that extraordinary, never-repeated day at the rental house, but we all knew a deep joy, an even greater marveling that is with me still.

AFTERWORD . . . WITH DR. JILL

"Honor thy father and mother . . ."?

Do we honor our parents because they are honorable, or because we want to be people who are honoring? We certainly do not honor dishonorable acts. But if we each can separate the person from his or her behavior, we can honor at least the fact that our parents helped bring us into this world and that they occupy the roles of mother or father in our lives. Just as we honor the role of president, even if we did not vote for him and may even be vehemently opposed to his policies, we give honor to his elected position of authority.

When considering appropriate honor, should we honor others, even parents, when they continue their wayward ways? Does bad behavior deserve our honor? No way! Honor does not mean we regress to our child status and give wrong-acting parents power over us. Especially now as growing and grown children, we must learn to set boundaries around their dishonorable behavior. We do not allow them to be with us, or our own kids, in ways that are unacceptable. They do not get to rage at us, abuse us, or show up drunk on holidays.

Setting boundaries is, in fact, a way of *preserving* relationship with those who have hurt us. Boundaries are not steel doors slammed in a person's face, but rather, loving and firm ways of saying no, not now, not here. Setting boundaries honors both people involved by not allowing either one to dishonor the other or the relationship through unacceptable words or actions.

This ability to establish boundaries when necessary with our parents means we've entered a level of more mature functioning. Honor and boundaries go together; we cannot have one without the other. When we take care of ourselves and are adults who choose to act rightly, that brings honor to our parents. Traditional Eastern cultures understand this idea of bringing honor or dishonor to our family name through our actions. If your parents are dishonorable, find what you *can* honor, no matter how small. Giving honor is a choice you make to be a person of honorable behavior. Such honor helps your own heart and gives honor to your Father in heaven.

Others can help us heal and lead us to honoring actions and thoughts. Joy, whom we met in the last chapter, helped Jimmy heal through the love and security she gave him. In kind, Jimmy could give to his father because he wanted to, not because he needed to. Not all of us have such a person in our lives; should we perhaps begin our own twelve-step group, called Adult Children of the Dishonorable?

It can be hard to face our parents' behaviors on our own. And often there is a generational cycle at work: there are many prodigal parents who were once children of prodigal parents, and on and on it goes. We often choose to run from these truths, but it ends up compounding our misery. We're not sure we can bear what we may know intuitively but aren't ready to know cognitively.

When your parent is a prodigal raised by a prodigal, you fear there is something wrong with you, that you are truly unlovable. It is hard to tease out what is us and what is them and what keeps getting passed on through the generations—and perhaps even through our biology. However, even with our genetics we bear the responsibility to find out and learn what we can. Otherwise, it is like the person who knows that cancer runs in her family but doesn't go to the doctor when she feels a lump or a pain, in order to avoid bad news. Then she becomes terminally ill because she didn't catch it soon enough. We honor ourselves and others by letting ourselves know.

Leslie had suspicions about her father. She bravely sought out information that would help her honor him for who he was in the context of his history, his behavior, and his oddities. I think she pegged pretty accurately the man she called Father, the one she knew but didn't know. Schizoid traits and features and/or full-blown personality disorder was my bet prior to reading her findings thus far in her story. It is a small percentage of the population, comparatively, that have a diagnosable personality disorder. The more fixed, rigid, and pervasive character symptoms are, the farther down the continuum to a personality disorder a person is. There is a lot written on the schizoid traits beyond diagnostic symptomology. Many who write from a psychoanalytic or psychodynamic orientation give rich understanding to the complexities of this seemingly more removed, self-contained, self reliant, self-preserved personality constellation. And yet, most notably, personality disordered individuals are some of the most difficult to treat. The poor prognosis is partly due to the resistance to recognize the need for treatment, the resources to sustain the longer-term therapy needed, and the slow, arduous progress and limited results.

Lest we be discouraged to leave our prodigal here, alongside our knowing reality about human limitations, we can also hold on to our faith-based knowledge that all things are possible with God. God's desire to love and reclaim the people He has created, regardless of their genetics or abilities, is beyond our comprehension.

God's ways are not ours, nor are His views of healing. Even in Jesus' day, people wanted a glorious savior, not a suffering servant. Remember how they mocked Jesus, laughingly naming him King of the Jews? They did not understand God's master plan for our redemption.

What if *you* could be a part of your parent's redemption? All things *are* possible with God. Allow Him to use you and you may just see a sin forgiven, a heartbreak healed, a relationship restored— and a parent honored.

Study Questions

1. What does honor mean to you? First, just allow yourself to think, without any person in mind, of the idea, concept, and action of *honor.*

2. Reread Romans 12:18. Let's break it down into three parts for examination. If we were to turn each phrase into a question, how would you respond? First, circle or highlight the word(s) that is the emphasis of each phrase below. Now try responding to these phrases as if they were questions.
   · *If it is possible?* _____
   · *As far as it depends on you?* _____
   · *Live at peace with everyone?* _____

3. Now consider the above passage with your personal situation.
   · *Is it possible in my situation to be at peace with my parent(s)?*
   · *What or how much depends on me?*
   · *Who is "everyone"? How is "live at peace" qualified by the two preceding phrases?*

4. Name some examples of honorable behavior that you try to live

out in your own life. In what ways have you felt treated honorably by others?

5. List some characteristics from the honorable examples you named above. Where did your honorable values come from?

6. How do honor and boundaries go together? Are honor and respect the same thing? If I honor a person, do I also respect his or her rights to personal boundaries?

7. Are there some boundaries that need to be set in order for you to have an honorable adult relationship with your parent(s)? What ideas come to mind?

8. Practice writing how you might verbally express your boundary with your father or mother. (For example, "Thanks, Mom, but _____ is not going to work for me.") The directness and severity of your boundary will depend on your specific situation and the degree of communication you have with your parent(s).

9. Pray about your willingness to be an honorable person for your heavenly Father. Tell God all the dishonorable things your earthly parents have done. It's okay—He's heard and seen it all, but for you it may do you good to cry on His massive shoulders. Then ask Him to show you how to be honorable in the face of dishonor. If you are willing, write a prayer to God offering your will to be honoring in His eyes.

10. You have told God and others the ways in which your parents have acted dishonorably. But can you name one way they were kind to you? What if you start there and begin shifting from praying about their hurtful ways toward you to incorporating praying for your parents and their healing?

Lord, Have Mercy:
In the Last Hours

And why all this ardor if death is close? . . .
What continents, what oceans, what a show it is!
In the hall of pain, what abundance on the table.
—Czeslaw Milosz[1]

ED DOBSON, A pastor for many years and the author of *A Year of Living Like Jesus,* stands on a boardwalk overlooking a pond. He is holding a sheet of paper with a list of names, the people he knows he has offended in his life and in his ministry. On some of the issues dividing them, he is sure he was the aggrieved party, but he has decided that restoring the relationship is more important than who was right and who was wrong. He will either write letters or visit them one by one to ask for their forgiveness.

It is painful to watch the short video of this experience.[2] Ed has Lou Gehrig's disease and is a walking skeleton. He was supposed to die ten years ago, but he has lived on for another twelve years, his body wasting away.

Don't we wish our fathers or our mothers, or both, would

come to our doors with a humble knock and a yearning to make things right? How many of the dying do this? How many clear their accounts, confess mistakes, ask for forgiveness before their final departures? It happens in the movies.

In *Get Low*, Robert Duvall plays Felix Bush, an old man with a secret—a secret that has sent him alone into the woods as a hermit. He is hostile to the people of the nearby town and feared by the children. For forty years he hides in the woods, forgoing marriage, children, the usual joys of life. We don't find out until near the end why he is there: he is punishing himself for his sins.

When his heart weakens and he knows he'll die soon, he decides it's time to confess. He arranges for his own funeral party to be held on his land, with him in attendance. In the gathering of hundreds of curious town folk, he mounts the wooden stage built for the occasion and speaks into the microphone, haltingly at first, then with increasing confidence. He confesses the sin that has driven him from all company:

"I did something I was ashamed of and could never fix. When I told Charlie what I'd done, he told me to confess to God and the law to what I'd done. I didn't want forgiveness. I needed to hold on to it to make me sick. You see, I fell in love with a married lady. The only time I've been in love. We were to run off together, start a new life, a new family . . ."

He pauses, breathes heavily, then describes what happened that night forty years ago. He was to meet up with his paramour outside her house, but when he got there, the house was on fire. He ran inside, and she was crawling on the floor, her head bleeding. She'd been hit by her husband with a hammer when he discovered her plan. Husband and wife both died in the fire; Felix alone escaped.

He ends his confession, "It came to me clear. It was all my fault . . . I'm so ashamed, so ashamed . . . I would like forgiveness now, if possible. I don't mind dying for real. Please forgive me."

He died not many days after, at peace finally with himself and with the people he had harmed so grievously.[3]

We don't require quite so much drama, but we would like even a small acknowledgment from our parents of their own part in the "universal disaster of sinful brokenness."[4] (See chapter 3.) We have surely played a part in it as well, but a few words from them would make such a difference. If they have resisted such words all their lives, surely when they are old, when death is on the way, there will be some kind of settling of accounts. (And we are not the only ones who wait in hope. There are just as many loving, good parents hoping their children will come and say the same words to them, confessing their own failings and wrongs, asking forgiveness.) As long as there is breath, there is hope for truth-telling, forgiveness, and reconciliation.

But we cannot place our hopes in our parents. A mother *can* come knocking at our door, a father *can* make that phone call, but most times it does not happen. The years go by. And now we are older, knowing it is time to stop waiting for them. Perhaps by now they are elderly and diminishing. Or they are not old yet, but they are sick, maybe even dying. What will we do now?

If we have not done it by now, it is time to shift whatever love we have for our parents from "Need-love" to "Gift-love," a distinction C. S. Lewis made in his book *The Four Loves*.[5] We're born into our parents' arms—we cannot live without them. We love them through our needs, a love that depends upon the other for life, health, and well-being. As our parents age, they return to our arms and are often as needy and dependent upon us as we once were upon them. We may still need their love, but as we've matured, we hope to grow toward a deeper kind of love, Gift-love, based on the simple desire to give and love another regardless of our own needs and the other's response. This is how God loves us.

Is it possible to move from Need-love to Gift-love now, when our parents need us most?

It's not easy. We are struck with so many conflicting emotions. I would look at my father asleep on his bed and remember the doctor's words: "He has congestive heart failure. He has only a few months to live." I felt pity at his weakened state, his frail body. Anger at who he was, at how different we were, fearful of him dying, compassion for his pain.

Gayle stood by her father's bed rails, gazing on him with little feeling. He was unconscious and unlikely to wake up. She had not been able to forgive him, had not even thought of it yet. After all he had done. Could she forgive him now?

Vonnie made her way shakily to her mother's bedroom. Her mother, her abuser. Should she forgive her now, days before her death? What was the point?

It feels so unjust. These parents had no idea of the anguish they had caused. They were about to leave behind all the wreckage they'd created while everyone in their path is left fingering their scars. *Do they even need my forgiveness? They're going to stand before God and give an account to Him—they need God's forgiveness a lot more than they need my forgiveness!* Such are our thoughts. Mercy can falter and stall even here at the last.

Who will show us the way in the final hours?

There is one man who has shown us the way. In His own last hours, staked by His feet and hands, and hoisted above the heads of His tormentors, He did not leave this world silently. From that bloody mount, with stabbing pain simply to breathe, He spoke. His first words—what were they? Not curses for His enemies and executioners, like the man hanging next to Him. Neither did He justify and defend Himself. Nor did He scream for His own deliverance. He prayed, but not even for Himself. In the midst of His encmies' gloating and their glad satisfaction at the extermination of their rival, Jesus rasped out, loud enough for them to hear, "Father, forgive them, for they don't know what they are doing" (Luke 23:34).

Did they catch their breath? Were their own hearts pierced? It was the least likely time to offer forgiveness. In the midst of Jesus' greatest pain. When surrounded by His executioners. He was the least likely person to utter those words: He was innocent, guilty only of healing and feeding and raising the dead. In their greatest hour of guilt, and therefore their greatest hour of need, Jesus offered what he knew they needed most: the possibility of forgiveness. Jesus would not let their guilt be the final word. "Father, forgive them . . ."

They could kill Him—for a few days—but they could not stop Him from doing what He had come for: to love and to offer forgiveness, even in death.

Who can bear the weight of this scene? Who can contain the opposite poles of deepest hate and utmost love? How can human beings, mere dust and spit, hope to imitate such a life and such a death? But I know already, in our faulty, small human way, we can do this as well: in our parents' greatest hours of need, we can offer blessing instead of curses. No matter how difficult those hours are, deep moments of mercy and reconciliation can come, changing the course of *your* life, and changing the end of their lives.

By the time Vonnie, after months of seeing a counselor and equipping herself to face her abuser, stood by her mom, her siblings had already told her their mother was nearly gone. Vonnie's mom, in the final stages of Alzheimer's and near death, did not have much to offer Vonnie, but it was more than she expected. Her mom offered her a kind of apology. "I shouldn't have been so hard on you," she whispered.

Vonnie was ready. She had been working for months, perhaps even decades, toward this moment.

"It's okay, Mom. I forgive you," Vonnie responded, her hand on her mother's.

Vonnie returned to her mother's deathbed two more times and was there for her last day. She was almost unrecognizable, just eighty pounds and white-haired. Vonnie sat beside her and ran her fingers through her hair; she touched her feet. She gave her mother something that her mom had never had before—a loving touch. As she touched her, she spoke soothingly, "I want you to know I forgive you and I love you." It was one of the biggest moments in Vonnie's life. The burden she had been carrying since childhood, that had only gotten heavier over time, was finally lifted. She knew her mother still had to face God, but Vonnie released her from her own judgment and was then freed to care for her needs. And she knew her mother needed her presence and prayers. The hospice nurse had told Vonnie that her mother had been having nightmares, screaming that there was something dark and scary in her room. Despite her mother's decades-long abuse of her, Vonnie was afraid for her and wanted to be there to comfort her. She hoped that if her mother knew she had forgiven her, she would be freed to ask God for forgiveness too. In those last few days, Vonnie felt a new, deep concern for her mother's well-being, a concern that was a balm for her own heart as well.

We don't always get last words, even small admissions of guilt or regret. By the time Gayle arrived at her father's hospital bed rail, he was already unconscious. He wouldn't even know she was there. But it wasn't too late. She stood in his room, looking at her siblings and her mother, amazed—amazed that they had all gone to such trouble to gather around a man whose one talent seemed to be ruining their every family event. One had flown all the way from Saudi Arabia. She herself had flown from Alaska.

He had been paranoid schizophrenic, had even been institutionalized at several points. Gayle had so many bad memories. He had ruled like a tyrant and hadn't allowed Gayle or her siblings to bathe when he was home. They'd had to wash their hair and take baths secretly, so he wouldn't rage about the water they were using. Loud laughter was not allowed. There was to be no joy, no noise in his home. But Gayle had come to be with him in his final hours. They weren't a close family, they did not find solace in each other, but there they were, talking, holding hands, and praying for him as he lay before them.

Later that day, Gayle arranged to be alone with him in the ICU. She came prepared.

Holding onto the bed rails, looking down at his unmoving form, she spoke. "I am really mad at how unfair you were, Daddy. I did not appreciate not being able to laugh. It was very hard. We were walking on eggshells all the time, and it was wrong! But I forgive you and I love you."

Later, Gayle sat in my living room, describing the scene from twenty years ago:

> I believe he heard me. When my brother walked in right after
> my time with him, the heart monitor fluttered. But I did not
> feel the words I spoke. I didn't feel love. I didn't feel any yearn-
> ing for forgiveness. I knew, totally by faith, that someday God
> would heal me further, and I knew that I would later wish I had
> said those words. So I said them in faith, knowing that someday
> I would feel those words more. I didn't want my father to con-
> tinue to ruin my life. I didn't want him shutting off forgiveness
> in other areas of my life, and controlling me out of the grave.
> They weren't magic words, but I believed that saying them would
> begin the way into them. And it's happened. There's been a lot
> of healing since then.

Our forgiveness is not God's forgiveness, however. We know that. As Miroslav Volf reminds us in *Free of Charge*, all of our forgiveness is hopelessly incomplete in itself. "Our forgiving is faulty; God's is faultless. Our forgiving is provisional; God's is final. We forgive tenuously and tentatively; God forgives unhesitatingly and definitively. We often even wrong the other by misjudging the offense, but God forgives with justice and genuine love."[6] Of course, our forgiveness won't slip them past an having to account for themselves to God. But it will save them from our own con-demnation. Our witness of mercy will powerfully illuminate the forgiveness of God that awaits them even then, if they so choose. The cycle of receiving only what is deserved is broken.

We all dread the last years of our parents' lives: the declin-ing health, the diminishment of capabilities, the loss of selfhood, the responsibilities that come uninvited to the grown children. It's particularly hard for the ones whose parents were not nurturing. But there are unexpected mercies that can come even through this process.

Deanna, a pastor's wife, never dreamed she would attend her father's every health crisis in the last few years of his life. Why would she? He had been a harsh, angry man who imposed and enforced such rigid rules upon his wife and seven children that they lived in fear of him. Even in the care facility, he lashed out with his cane, hitting his own caregivers at will until they took his cane away. The older Deanna got, the angrier she got, recognizing more and more how much harm he had done to her and her siblings. Yet she was there at his side consistently through the dying process.

What brought her there? After years of struggling to forgive him, finally, in her fifties, when a speaker came to her church, Deanna was able to release him from her anger.

I finally understood that forgiveness was not saying what the person did was okay, but it meant to release them from your own judgment to God's judgment. You're getting out of the way and releasing judgment to where it belongs, to God. The whole process of his illness was God's grace to him and to us as a family. My dad always had to be in control. He had to be in control at all times. He finally had to submit to other people caring for him, calling the shots. It was a very painful process. But even at the end, even when he couldn't speak, I felt the most loved by my dad then than I ever did before. He would just look at us with these eyes and try to reach out for our hands. And be very obviously glad we were there. In those last days, I finally felt loved by my father. I'm so glad I was there.

However hard and grace-filled those months and days of attending an ill parent are, not everyone is given this chance. Sheryl's father ended his own life when she was nineteen. He drove to the doctor's office and asked the receptionist repeatedly to talk to the doctor. She said the doctor wasn't available. So he asked to use their restroom. He then went into the bathroom and shot himself.

Sheryl was shopping for a dress with her boyfriend, Donald, when her mother, frantic to find her, called the store. Donald took the message. He did not tell her about her father right there in the store.

On the way home, he pulled the car over and told her about her father's suicide. She didn't believe him. She thought it was a joke. How could this be? She never had the chance to work through her complicated relationship with her father, a controlling man whom she feared, yet still loved.

My own story of my last hours with my father did not turn out well.

It was the last day of my ten-day visit, the day after we brought him to our rental house in Florida. My brother Todd and I sat with him in his room, a small, rectangular space with just enough room for a bed, a stuffed chair, and a small bookcase with books on astronomy, science, and travel, books he could no longer read. On the wall over his bed hung a blanket with a Northern landscape and a wolf. A few oil landscapes hung on the other walls.

Todd was saying good-bye. His last good-bye. He knew he would not come again, no matter what happened next. It was a long way from Alaska to Florida, and he had six children he could not easily leave. I hoped I could come when the end came, but I had no assurance I would be able to. We all knew my dad could not live much longer, that he had already outlived the doctor's assessment of his heart. It was weak. It could go anytime, he told my sister six months ago.

My father sat on the bed, his legs over the edge, his feet on the floor. He was tired. With his heart so weak, I knew he never got the full oxygen he needed. But Todd and I did not want to leave without saying something about our lives, some kind of summation, some kind of blessing. How to do this?

"That was a busy time, wasn't it, Dad? You must be tired after everyone being here," I offered.

He smirked slightly, without eye contact, "My fifteen minutes of fame."

Todd and I laughed, reminded again how much more present he was than he appeared. I saw Todd take a breath.

"Dad, remember when we were growing up? We had such hard times . . ." Todd was sitting on one side of my father; I sat in front of him. Todd sat leaning forward just slightly, being careful to give his attention without overwhelming him. He spoke softly, with pauses between phrases so Dad could follow. "We all left, scattered as soon as we could. We were not much of a family. But God has made us a family again. God brought us all together." Todd's eyes were bright. I blinked back tears.

My father sat, owlish, on the bed, looking vacantly at Todd. He was clearly bored. He said nothing in response.

My brother and I exchanged deep, pleading looks. We didn't know what to say or how to do what we knew we needed to.

"I just want to say that I'm glad I got to see you, that I love you, and that I'll be praying for you, Dad," I said finally, to end the long silence.

He blinked, pressed his mouth into a mild, impatient smirk. He did not want to hear about God or prayer.

Todd plunged forward gently. "I don't know if I'll get to see you again . . . I just want to say good-bye, Dad. I'll be praying for you too."

He tilted his head to the side, expressionless, clearly waiting for us to be done, then looked down at his watch. It was nearly dinnertime. He was thinking about dinner, not about saying good-bye to his children. I sighed and signaled to Todd, pointing to my watch. He nodded slowly.

"Well, Dad, it looks like it's time for dinner. Do you want to go down to the dining hall now?"

He lifted his head, his eyes brightened, and he reached for his walker. I grabbed it from the corner, and Todd helped him stand.

"We'll walk down with you, Dad."

We shuffled out of the room and down the hallway, Todd on one side, me on the other, my father bent over his walker, taking six-inch steps at a time, his ankles and legs swollen. It took several minutes to get to our destination on this slow train. I felt utterly defeated.

We entered the dining hall, an alcove fitted with round tables, seating four to six per table. All the residents were already there. I saw Sally, my friend, with her arthritis-gnarled hands. She smiled and nodded at me. She was one of Dad's smoking partners who had joined him out in the smoking shed every day, cigarettes in hand, before his stroke. They would talk about God, Sally said. "Your father says he's an atheist," she told me on one of my visits.

"Yes, I know. He's told me that for twenty years."

"But I'm telling him about the Lord," she said brightly. "We stand out there in the smoking shack, Billy and me and one other guy, and we talk about God."

I laughed, envisioning this, sharing cigarettes and God in the back of a nursing home.

I saw the woman who was always perfectly made up, who looked no more than sixty-five, and who sat at the table so patiently, regally, while she waited twenty minutes for a plate of hot dogs and canned peaches. I saw Jeanette, the ninety-four-year-old woman who walked the parking lot every day for exercise. David in the wheelchair, and Billy, who was only in his sixties but who had lost his memory entirely.

They all watched as Todd and I cleared the way for Dad to get to his table. He sat at the back of the room, the table by the mirrored wall, and faced the mirror, his back to his fellow residents. His food was already there, hot dogs and beans, his favorite. I took the walker while he carefully eased himself down to the chair. Todd and I hovered, not knowing what to do. We wanted to help; we wanted to change everything that was happening. We wanted to love him in a way he would see and hear, that would penetrate his thick chest—and we wanted him to send love back to us.

We looked at each other over his head, and we knew we would not stay. We knew he would not talk or want company while he ate. As soon as he was seated, he was eating, all eyes and attention on his food. He seemed to have forgotten we were there.

"Well, Dad . . ." Todd began. "I guess we need to go. This is, ummm, this is . . . good-bye."

My father did not look up from his plate.

I tried. "Dad, I'm so glad we got to spend these days with you. It's been so good to be with you. I hope to see you again, but I don't know if I can." I paused to see if there would be any response. He was chewing his beans slowly and carefully, since he had no teeth.

"So . . . I love you, and I will be praying for you, Dad." I sighed.

"So . . . good-bye, Dad." I leaned down, kissed his head, hugged his shoulders as best I could.

He did not look up at us. He didn't acknowledge our presence in any way. Todd and I looked at each other and turned to go. We stepped away from his table heavily, waiting for a word to turn us back. It came, but not from him. Sally, Billy, Jeanette, others whose names we didn't know but whom we had talked with, called out, waving to us.

"Good-bye!"

"It was so good to see you again!"

"Have a safe trip back home!

"Thanks for coming!"

"God bless you!"

We turned and smiled and waved back, and my heart was gladdened for a second, that they had seen us and were glad for our coming and were blessing our leaving. But the words were spoken by the wrong people.

Todd and I walked out the sliding doors, our steps leaden. In those ten days with him, taking him to our house, bringing him out for ice cream, filling his room with our presence and memories, he did not acknowledge any wrongs. He did not ask for forgiveness. I did not expect any of this. But he did not speak my name once. Nor did he thank any of us for coming. He would not even say good-bye.

Those were my last hours with my father. *Do I forgive him of this?* I wondered. *Is this self-absorption and the hurt it delivered—was this covered in my previous forgiveness? Does his schizoid personality disorder excuse this?* It began again: I remembered his mental illness, remembered how weak his heart was. I rehearsed what I was learning: that we will all keep hurting one another—mental illness or not. That is part of what it means to be human, and part of what it means to be in a family. That we all owe huge debts to God, yet they have been paid and covered. I had been freed by another Father who loved me purely, who loved me entirely, who knew my name. I felt a deep sense of consolation, yet I could not fully end my sadness.

When the call came two months later that my father had stopped eating and was close to death, I was teaching at a ten-day residency in Santa Fe. I was walking to a meeting with a student when my cell phone rang. It was Laurie. "Hospice called and said Dad is conscious. He is sitting in the chair, but he has stopped eating. They advised me to get there as soon as possible. I can get there tomorrow morning. Can you come?"

I could not let those minutes in that dining room be my last hours with my father. Though I'd left that day determined not to come again, I knew instantly I had to be there one last time. I went online that afternoon and found the cheapest ticket; a flight to Orlando and then a return to Kodiak was three thousand dollars. And I could only stay two and a half days. Less than three days, three *thousand* bucks, and my husband and children, who did not know my father except for that one meeting, asking me to come home. Begging me to come home. Over the next twenty-four hours, between classes and students, I wrung my hands, paced the driveway, prayed wordlessly to the heavens. I had been gone from home for almost two weeks already. But I promised Laurie she wouldn't have to go through his death alone. Clark had come and was with her, but I desperately wanted to be there as well. In my fear and exhaustion, with the cost of the ticket and my young children at home, I did not go.

I did not go.

The next evening of the residency was graduation for the students who had finished the MFA program. Just before the ceremony, I called Laurie again, knowing I would be unavailable for the next hour or two. He was still alive, still unconscious, still laboring for breath, Laurie told me. I asked her to hold the phone to his ear so I could tell him I loved him. I could hear his constricted breathing. "I love you, Dad, and I hope I'll see you in heaven." Just his whistling breath. I finished with Laurie and hung up abruptly.

I entered the festive room white-faced, shaking, and took my seat with the faculty. Among the music, speeches, and cheer, I sat in my chair gasping for air, a hand over my chest to keep my heart in place. I was supposed to give the closing benediction. I could not speak grace over anyone that day. I could not speak at all.

These were my last hours before my father's death. Laurie and Clark's last hours with our father were quiet as well. When they arrived at his room in the nursing home, he was in bed, unresponsive. To Laurie, he looked like a little boy, helpless, his hair disheveled in sleep. They read scriptures to him. Laurie stroked his hair, his head, told him she loved him, that it was okay for him to go now. His face would change expression; he seemed to be responding. But the hours were heavy. She thought of all he had done, how he had used her as a girl. She wanted to wipe away those years. She hated him for how her life had gone for so many years after because of him, but there was love there too. He had asked for her forgiveness two years before in a phone call. He'd told her she was a beautiful person inside and out; she had a wonderful heart; he loved her, and would she forgive him? She had said yes. Not simply because he asked. Laurie meant it. She had been talking to him on the phone for three years by then. She had forgiven him before he asked, but his asking helped her to further release him from the wrongs he had done and freed him from repaying what could not be repaid.

Laurie went on to help him find a care facility, to help set him up in his room. Later, after his stroke, she found the rehab for him and took care of his finances. The abused loved the abuser and made sure he had a bed at night, meals every day, gifts at Christmas, and phone calls when he was alone, though he had done none of this for her, for any of us. He received it all, even appearing grateful occasionally, but he didn't understand it. He didn't understand why anyone was showing kindness to him. Especially Laurie.

The day passed into night this way: Laurie and Clark silently remembering, reading, touching Dad's head and hands, praying. Finally, unable to keep awake, Laurie left to find a couch to rest on while Clark remained, sitting by his bed. Hours later, when Dad's breath became irregular, Clark ran to find Laurie. Moments later, my father took his last shuddering breath; then the room fell silent.

Laurie sat in a kind of shock. Numb, she fixed his hair, folded his hands across his chest, kissed him on the cheek, and prayed he was with the Lord. For the next four hours, Laurie and Clark were there with our father's body, crying, talking. They found a photo album they hadn't seen before and began to look through it. They didn't know him. They didn't know what happened to him to make him the way he was. The hours passed.

Men came for him at 5:00 a.m., entering the room with a black bag. Laurie and Clark left the room as they put his body into the bag.

And I wasn't there. Lord, have mercy; I didn't go. I would do almost anything to take that back.

It was over now. My hope that he might speak to me, love me back in some small way. My hope of understanding him. All the letters and cards I had been sending, the prayers, the gifts, the phone calls, all this was done. There was no more mercy and love to be given—or to be received.

———

If you are lucky enough to get a call, I hope you will do better than me. I hope you will go. I hope you will go years before the calls start coming. Go before a mother or father lies unable to respond. But even if that time is now, go now. Don't miss this chance. Do it for your parent's sake. Each of the mothers and fathers in this chapter could have easily died alone. But instead they died in the company of people they had hurt but who gathered to love them and pray comfort and peace for them. Do it for your own sake.

Deanna tells me her forgiveness of her father and the love she received from him in his last days gave her the courage and confidence to leave nursing and finally do what she really desired to do: to become a women's pastor. Gayle's presence at her father's bedside, speaking those simple words, "I love you and I forgive you," began the way into a forgiveness that deepened over the years, toward healing, and has enabled her to forgive others. Laurie and Clark's attending of my father's passing gave them the closure they needed to look backward with kindness and to live at peace in the present.

I think of the man who died alone in a VA facility. The son, who called his father "just another despicable, nasty, old man," refused to come and identify the body. I didn't know the man who died, what he was really like. I am guessing the son did not know him either. Sadly, the chance to show compassion, to lessen the pain of dying by his simple presence, is gone. The chance for forgiveness and reconciliation is gone.

Most of all, as we each stand there with our parent, one essential question emerges: will we carry on the sins of our fathers and mothers, or will we break the generational cycle of destruction and selfishness? As Vonnie's mother lay on her deathbed, the hospice nurse turned to those gathered and said softly, professionally, "This would be a good time to share a nice memory of your mother." She looked around the room expectantly. Everyone there froze. No one spoke. In the silence that never ended, Vonnie vowed she would live a different life, a life that would not end in choked silence.

It is in the final hours that our decision becomes so clear: we *can* break free from the sins that so crippled our parents and their parents before them, however far back it goes. We can end the cycle ourselves with God's enabling. Yes, our children will leave our homes saddled with our imperfections and gaps as parents. And they will go on to have children with whom they will struggle. It is inevitable that every generation will do so—this is the human family. But this inevitability only highlights the constant, daily offering of forgiveness from God. We've been given all that we need to be whole people, people of peace, a forgiving people who won't allow others' sins to crush or smother us, who won't let our love be silenced by neglect and selfishness.

Our parents did not send us on our way with a blessing, but we can bless them as they leave. And in doing so, we begin a new legacy right now, ourselves, with or without our spouses, with or without our children's help, and now, of course, without our parents' help. They are gone. We are graduating from the limits of Need-love to the freedom of Gift-love. And we still have full and whole lives ahead to live.

Afterword . . . with Dr. Jill

Help! My parent is dying; how do I make things right? How do I let go of unfinished business? Death has a way of crystallizing in a moment what's most important, what we need or want, and what will never be.

When death is on the doorstep, there is an opening in our hearts, our minds, our understanding. It is like a portal where, through our sadness and tear-filled eyes, we see and feel a glimpse of beyond, of eternity. In those last moments we become aware and peeled down to the essence of what's most important in life. Those moments of understanding are sacred, and we carry them with us like precious gems.

Allowing ourselves to grieve is such an important piece of any healing journey. When we grieve, we are not running or avoiding; we are allowing the despair to flow over us and through us like a sieve that strains and refines our sadness. Grieving allows us to say those words, the ones we've always wanted to say. In the end, what we say, or sometimes what hangs in the silence of what we don't say, is important.

When my stepfather was dying from testicular cancer that had moved into his lungs, one hospital visit, I wanted to let him know how special he was to me. Having him in my life from age nine to seventeen made a big difference, especially against the backdrop of my intermittent biological dad. So I announced to him that I had decided I wanted him to be the one to walk me down the aisle someday when I got married. At seventeen, with marriage still an idealized fantasy, it was the greatest honor I could think of to bestow on a nonbiological father, and a resolve of my internal conflict as a child of divorce trying to make broken pieces fit. He looked at me and gave me that slight, knowing smile of his, just like my youngest brother gives, who is his only offspring, and with his dry-witted humor, he said, "Well, you probably should hurry up, then!" We laughed and I knew, even in my teenage awkwardness, that he knew I loved him, and that he loved me.

Being with and being present matters. There are no special, profound, or magic words—speaking from your heart what you've wanted to say is what matters. When it comes to the end of life, our sense of what's right often kicks in. We just need the courage to embrace the moment. And sometimes we need to fill in parts of our story that our parents cannot.

A friend of mine had a mother who was constantly in and out of the hospital from the time he was eight. As a result of her chronic health issues and accompanying emotional struggles, she was quite disconnected from him and highly critical of everything he did. She and his father fought constantly and would throw things at each other in his presence, not to mention the horrible things they would scream at each other. He felt heavily burdened as a child and was left to fend for himself throughout most of his adolescence. Receiving constant desperate calls from the hospital, he was always on edge, fearing she could die at any time. This went on for ten years, until at eighteen the final call did come, and he watched with ambivalence from her bedside as she passed into eternity.

Sadly, as an adult he still carried his critical, shaming mother inside his heart, her loud voice diffusing every good thing he did. He would try to assuage her words in his head by pleasing others as he sought the approval from them that he could never get from her. After a particularly difficult season when his mother issues were virtually screaming out of him and adversely affecting his life at home and at work, he asked me if I would go with him to visit his mother's grave. His therapist had suggested that he go and that he ask a trusted friend to go with him. He had not been there in years; in fact, he had purposely avoided going there since the day she was buried. We went, we sat, we prayed, and we lifted the negative hold his mother had on him to God and surrendered his resentment at her grave and at the foot of the cross. There was no music, no bright lights; it was simple but significant. He cried and cried, and then we left.

In the years following his mother's death, my friend mended and built a relationship with his father. In place of the years of anger, depression, and estrangement, it became one of shared respect and understanding. Through a relationship with Christ, a son's acts of forgiveness toward his father elicited a humble response from his dad that led to reconciliation.

We do our part by working our lives through to a point of being able to offer forgiveness, in our hearts and through our actions. Whether the other, our parent, responds to allow reconciliation to be possible is not up to us. We follow God's leading and know that "a soft answer turns away wrath" (Prov. 15:1 NKJV), but we cannot move our parents' hardened hearts to soften. However, God can use us when we get our own obstacles out of the way. In my friend's case, his grateful father has worked at making restitution for his neglect, and together they have grieved over my friend's lost childhood.

While it was indeed a happier end, it was still far from idyllic. Hurt and pain take their toll, and only when a person chooses God above all else and forgives the sins of the father is there a chance for something better than brokenness. My friend and his father, though long-distance, now talk every day by phone.

Gift-love versus Need-love is a higher road, a higher calling. Not all can take it. It is choosing to love in spite of, not because of, our parents. We can only do this when our lives and our whole emotional beings no longer depend on theirs. This does not mean we no longer yearn to hear loving words from them, or that it wouldn't be healing to finally receive something good; it means that we have surpassed our daily need for their affirmation. We have let go of expectation and allowed others into our lives who offer something different. We find safety and comfort elsewhere and know that we can and will be okay—with or without our longed-for parental response.

Study Questions

1. Who have you lost in your life, through death or long-term estrangement, whom you were close to? List all significant people, whether a parent or not.
2. Consider how the endings or last words with people you've lost affected you long after their departure.
3. Take a moment to recall your last exchange or experience with your departing parent. Do you remember—can you picture it? Do you remember what you told yourself about that exchange?
4. If you could have a *redo*, one more day or even hour with that parent, what would you do, not do, or say differently? What do you imagine that opportunity might bring you?
5. Even if, and especially if, your parent is gone, forgiveness is important for you to move beyond the grave. What steps or actions can you take to release the bondage your deceased

or absent parent has on you and thus allow yourself to rest in peace long after your parent is gone?

6. What was the one thing you felt like you never got from your parent? Did you grieve the loss of that experience? How are you going to own it now? What ways are you able to find this loss fulfilled in the present parts of your life?

7. What was your favorite memory of your parent? Was there a moment in time when you connected? (It is possible for some that this question will have no answer.)

8. When a parent dies, the hope of reconciliation with that parent dies too. Have you grieved your lost hopes and expectations? After death, hope can properly transfer to an eternal reconciliation where God heals all brokenness and deals lovingly and justly with each of us. Are you able to see your parent's humanness and brokenness?

9. What were your expectations of your parent while he or she was still here? Were they reasonable given what you know of your parent now? Do you have those same expectations in your own parenting? Do you meet them?

10. What is it that your deceased parent has finally found peace from? What was the darkness in his or her life that stood in the way of the joy of having a good relationship with you? How do you reconcile what you thought to be true and what you know is real now?

EIGHT

AFTER LAMENT: RECLAIMING THE PAST

It's never too late to have a happy childhood.
—TOM ROBBINS[1]

Forgiving does not erase the bitter past. . . . Instead, forgiving what we cannot forget creates a new way to remember. We change the memory of our past into a hope for our future.
—LEWIS B. SMEDES[2]

WE ARE ON the beach, Laurie, Clark, and I. It's June, ninety-five degrees, with 90 percent humidity, the air so heavy I can hardly breathe. The ocean is gray and quiet. We walk limply, languid in the heat, each of us carrying a Ziplock bag of ashes in our pockets. We have only two days together, but we're glad we've got even that. It's taken us three months since our father died to return to Florida to do this.

This was not our plan for the day. We were going to rent kayaks and launch onto a river to scatter his ashes where they would find their way to the sea. But by the time we found the rental place, it was close to closing. We did not want to be rushed. The beach, then, would suffice.

We walk slowly onto the beach, the sand here not brilliant white, like Crystal Beach in Sarasota, the beach we visited with my father five years ago. This one is beige, nondescript, but empty of people, which makes it perfect.

When Laurie and I arrived at Clark's house that morning, we took the heavy, brown-papered package off his shelf with wonder and dread. Clark had waited for us to come before opening it. To hold what was left of our father in our hands—what so many have done before us, but for us, the first time. The heft of it surprised me, maybe ten pounds. Even in death, my father was weighty. We opened the box together. The paper slipped off the wooden box; then a clasp opened to a smaller box inside. That box was screwed tight, sending Clark foraging for a Phillips screwdriver. Finally, we peered into gray powder in the plastic-lined box—all that a fiery furnace left from a life, a body. We took turns with a spoon, carefully scooping ashes into our own Ziplock bags, then sealing them, stowing them in our pockets, our hands shaking slightly with reverence, a sense of the holy.

We have no script for this day, a day marked as a funeral. There will be no service for him. Who would come? What would we say? The only one I know who calls herself a friend is Sally at the nursing home. But a life, any life, cannot end without acknowledgment. Someone has to say, *This was Howard Leyland. He was a man. He was alive. He gave life to six others. He was our father. His life mattered. His death matters.* We will say those things. To remember.

"Do you remember the summer nights we would all go out

onto the lawn and do wheelbarrow races, stand on our heads, and play leapfrog? Sometimes Dad would come out and watch us."

"Did he tell you about his conversion story, how he came to believe in UFOs?" And we laugh, comparing versions of the story.

We keep walking, kicking the sand at our feet.

"He was never mean to us," Clark says.

Laurie does not speak about his nightly visits.

I say nothing about his departures, his obliviousness to us, and how hard he would hit with his belt.

"I would have taken care of him. I wanted him to move next door."

Moments pass between each thought. Seagulls keen above us. We keep walking, each step both wandering and deliberate.

"Did you see the photo of Dad with that woman, before he was married? He had a girlfriend!"

"What else didn't we know about him?"

We are quiet, considering this.

"Remember how he would read the newspaper to us? I would be so annoyed that he couldn't talk to us, but we had to listen to him read."

We pick up shells, take photos of a great blue heron who stands motionless until we are just feet from him.

"He loved the ocean, but he couldn't sail."

"All those years dreaming about sailing around the world."

"I wonder if he was happy."

"How would anyone know if he was happy?"

"At least he got to live on the water for a while."

An hour passes. We sift memories between our hands, the anger long gone. We are sad for him, so little joy in his life. We are sick with the heat, but it is time. None of us knows how to turn us toward what must be done next. We grew up without ceremony or celebration. And we are Protestants without liturgies—just necessities. We stop walking, finally, face each other, and nod.

"Let's walk into the water," Clark says.

We wade into the salty suds up to our knees, the water as warm as our blood.

I pull out a folded paper. "Before we open the bags, I would like to read something," I say. It's part of Psalm 145, verses I have turned to many times. We stand together in the hot sun, in the hot salt water, and I begin:

> The Lord is trustworthy in all he promises
> and faithful in all he does.
> The Lord upholds all who fall
> and lifts up all who are bowed down. . . .
> The Lord is near to all who call on him,
> to all who call on him in truth.
> He fulfills the desires of those who fear him;
> he hears their cry and saves them. (vv. 13–14, 18–19)

I don't know if my father feared God at the last or called out to Him, at least in his mind and heart. But these words are for us. We hold hands, we cry, I pray, and we step away from one another to our own circles of ocean, each to the task of opening our bags, lifting, scattering, pouring, returning these pieces of body and bone to the element my father loved most.

We are nearly finished, but not yet. We are not done remembering, lamenting. The long, slow walk back, we talk again, more, filling in so many years of silence between us, filling in the years we were absent to one another, that our father was absent to us.

Finally, we return to the car, spent. With what energy we have left, we find a beachside restaurant and eat our dinner together, mostly quiet, but we know that the words and memories between us will not end here.

———————

None of this is extraordinary or remarkable. But it is ours, the lives we have lived because of our father, the death he has died: this is our particular burden of memories, and we are responsible for doing something with them, allowing them to shape our lives in the directions they should go. We know intuitively that "forgive and forget" won't do, that forgetting is a false hope at best. Forgiveness requires remembrance. We cannot confess and name what was done without memory. Neither can we extinguish what happened in the past by simply pretending or denying it away. We are time-bound beings. We wear memories in our faces, in the whorls and folds of our brains; we bear scars and burns on our bodies. Even when we desire to give up the memories that have formed us and even haunt us—we cannot. Nor should we. Patricia Hampl urges us to remember because, "we do not . . . simply have experience; we are entrusted with it. We must do something—make something—with it. A story, we sense, is the only possible habitation for the burden of our witnessing."[3]

We know this as a country. We spend billions to remember wars, the Holocaust, the attack on the World Trade Center. The more traumatic the event, the more we are charged to remember. If we do not remember where we have been as a nation, we will no longer know who we are.

Even the one, the only one, who is able to erase and heal all

His past wounds will not do so. At the end of tim restored, Jesus will return not healed but wounded ings on His hands and side strikingly visible. He is not a Savior without His death-dealing wounds. He is not a Comforter without the traumas He has borne. Why would we choose an emptied past over a healed, reclaimed one? We will remember, then, but we are charged to remember in a certain way, to "remember well," as L. Gregory Jones asserts in *Forgiving as We've Been Forgiven*.[4]

There are many guides to help us remember well. Frederick Buechner, well-known novelist and memoirist, is one of them. In his four-book memoir series, he has mined a complicated life. As a child, he moved virtually every year to a new city, a new school, with different people taking care of him each time. Then tragedy struck. When he was ten, his father took his own life through carbon monoxide poisoning. Buechner grew up under that shadow, becoming a Presbyterian minister and author. He knows the value—and the threat—of memories. We can easily be consumed by our own anger at the past and those who hurt us. Anger is decidedly "the most fun" of the seven deadly sins, Buechner tells us, tongue in cheek. "To lick your wounds, to smack your lips over grievances long past . . . to savor to the last toothsome morsel both the pain you are given and the pain you are giving back—in many ways it is a feast fit for a king. The chief drawback is that what you are wolfing down is yourself. The skeleton at the feast is you."[5]

We've all feasted at this banquet table. And after decades of dining on bones, smacking our lips over our parents' and others' sins that grow greater with each passing year, after such a dinner, what does this clacking, toothy lot of us do? We haul the same bones off to bed—our very own—huddling under the blankets: who did what to whom, and why, and how could they? Despite our heated, breathy recitations, which take all our strength, we are neither fed nor warmed. We must spend all our energies keeping these sickly creatures—our hurts and our grudges—alive, yet still we try.

There is no life, health, or rest to be found here. We know that by now. We must return to the past differently than we've been doing. The past can bring us wisdom and healing if we let it. As Buechner has written, "In everything that has happened to us over the years God was offering us possibilities of new life and healing which, though we may have missed them at the time, we can still choose and be brought to life by and healed by all these years later."[6]

We've begun to look behind us already. We've taken stock of our memories. We've looked with compassion upon our parents. We know that God's own forgiveness is offered to us, from the Father who stands on the hill, welcoming His prodigal daughter and son home. We know we are charged to forgive because we ourselves have been forgiven of everything. All of this is necessary and good.

But we cannot remember well without asking hard questions. We have already looked at how things have happened. As we considered our parents and their lives as children, how they became so wounded themselves, we began to understand the *how* of our own childhoods, but we haven't wrestled with the *why*. Why did these things happen to us? Maybe we haven't been encouraged to ask why, but we will find no peace without that question.

We ask it now. Why didn't we get the happy childhoods we deserved? Where were the apple trees and white fences and chocolate chip cookies after school, the mothers who tucked us in at night with prayers, the fathers who taught us to play baseball? Why did some get tossed back and forth between homes and stepparents? Why did others have to hide in fear from their fathers and run from their mothers? Why didn't God stop the abuse? Why did pain move in with us at such an early age?

Many times we don't know it, but our disappointments are often rooted in deeper assumptions, assumptions about the very meaning of our lives. We all want to live happy, fulfilled, comfortable lives. If we're American, we believe we were all born with the right to "Life, Liberty and the pursuit of Happiness."[7] Those of us who go to church regularly can get a double dose of this, unwittingly absorbing the notion not only that as Americans we get the American dream, but as Christians, we get God along with it, which makes our chances for happiness even better. We want and expect to be happy and blessed.

Larry Crabb, a best-selling psychologist, addresses this expectation in his book *Shattered Dreams: God's Unexpected Path to Joy*: "The problem sincere Christians have with God often comes down to a wrong understanding of what this life is most meant to provide. We naturally and wrongly assume we're here to experience something God never promised . . . We assume we are here for one fundamental reason: *to have a good time.*"[8] In *The Reason for God*, pastor Tim Keller identified the "basic premise of religion" as this: "that if you live a good life, things will go well for you."[9] But this premise is dead wrong, Keller asserts, reminding us what Jesus' own life looked like. He was the most morally pure person who ever lived, yet His life was filled with "poverty, rejection, injustice, and even torture."[10]

The question we must ask is larger than our own disappointment and pain. We must ask, is God in charge of this world—or not? And if He is, why does a good God allow such hard things in the lives of the youngest and most vulnerable?

In our heart of hearts, we may take on some of the blame

ourselves. We may believe it was our fault; *I did something wrong. I deserved it. I could have been a better child. I should have been smarter in school*, we think; *better in sports, more obedient.* Or we may blame God. We believe He is all-powerful, but He is not good. If He were good, wouldn't He have stopped the abuse? We may believe all kinds of lies about ourselves, about our parents, and about God, because we don't know how to reconcile our pain with a God of love.

I cannot answer in a few paragraphs the question of the ages, but we can get closer to the truth of who we are and who God is. He is the God who made us, who desires us, who loves us, who is not willing that any one of us should perish without Him. He is a God who is for us, not against us. He is the God who made both the light and the dark. "Though he brings grief, he will show compassion, so great is his unfailing love. For he does not willingly bring affliction or grief to the children of men" (Lam. 3:32–33). He is the God who allows us to choose our own paths, who witnessed our parents' choices—their alcoholism and neglect and anger and abandonment—with great sorrow. He has not been silent or inactive all the years of our sadness and frustration. He has been present during both the kindnesses and the hurts we received, leading and shepherding us toward Him, toward a better life.

I talked to Susan, a new friend, over lunch recently. Her mother was in a mental institution most of her childhood. Her father was in prison. She was raised for the first seven years of her life by a God-loving aunt and uncle who were so kind and loving she felt the presence of God through them. Though her family life descended into chaos and even torment when she left that home, she was forever marked by God's grace.

Though pain is ever present in most people's lives, it is not pain itself, finally, that diminishes us; it is our response to it that determines the kinds of lives we will live, the kinds of people we will be. We can choose a bitterness and an anger that will diminish us, or we can let our pain lead us toward God and one another. Without deep pain, psychologist Larry Crabb has found, we are unable to develop the capacity to recognize and enjoy true life. Pain is unavoidable in our lives, he wrote, but more than that, pain is "a necessary mile on the long journey to joy."[11]

Don't we know instinctively that this is true? These truths can change how we remember the past, and can alter its effects upon us even now, no matter how many years have gone by.

When Ruby was four, her sister was killed in an accident, an event Ruby remembers. Her parents' lives unraveled from there. By the time Ruby was ten, her mother had gone through twelve emotional breakdowns, leading finally to her parents' divorce. Ruby ended up living with her father. Ruby's mother became deeply depressed again, missing her daughter. Ruby was torn between households, living with her father and stepmother during the school week, and with her sad, needy mother during the weekends. While there, her mother would continually say, "I'm so depressed. No one loves me. Life isn't worth living."

When Ruby was sixteen, her mother attempted suicide and landed in the hospital, barely alive. Another family member was there, by her mother's door, talking to the police. He pointed over at Ruby. "That girl over there, it's her fault! She's the reason this happened!"

The night was not over yet. The doctor on call had just lost a patient and had no sympathy for Ruby or her mother. "Your mother may not make it through the night," he told Ruby brusquely. Then, with more anger, and to her face, "I just lost a patient who *wanted* to live."

How can so much grief and guilt be heaped upon a sixteen-year-old girl? Ruby was profoundly alone, with no help through those years and events.

I met her decades later over dinner. Ruby is vivacious, kind, outgoing. She is a counselor who leads a group on Tuesday nights for those who have lost a family member; she works with troubled children. As we dined, she described a trip to Nicaragua, where she ministered to women who were drug addicts. She knows about forgiveness, how it transforms the past. She shares her story with many, but she doesn't live in the past anymore. "I've learned and grown from it all," she told me. "I didn't want to travel that road of bitterness. I wanted to use those life experiences to help me grow stronger, to help me minister to others."

Allison Backous is spending a good part of her days immersed in the past. She is writing a memoir about her upbringing in an alcoholic, single-mother household, with poverty, dreariness, and hopelessness as her daily bread. In this work, she has come to the recognition that she must "remember well," that her return to the past must bless others: "But if I'm going to write, and if that is meant to bless others, then I had better acknowledge what is sacred about my past, my story. I had better write what I remember, not out of greed or malice, but out of seeking the true story, which includes blessing my mother, broken and afraid as she is. If I'm going to be a writer, I had better bless."[12]

I think of a man named Paul whose life was saturated with suffering. He was shipwrecked, beaten with a rod, imprisoned, under house arrest for years, and publicly whipped nearly to death three times. He lived constantly on the move and was in danger everywhere he went—in the city, in the country, on the sea—often traveling without enough food, clothing, and sleep. He lived this way for decades. I marvel at his physical endurance as I read his letters in the New Testament, yet I am even more astonished at his emotional endurance. He wrote about a life of such hardship, brutality, and persecution, and yet he wrote without bitterness or blame. He did not list the names of his persecutors or plot revenge against them. He was not consumed with the trials that became his life pattern as a follower of Christ, but he looked ahead to the future with confidence.

What did Paul do with so many enemies, with all those traumatic memories? How did he carry on throughout his trials without saddlebags of vengeance? After detailing his hardships, he told his readers the secret to his endurance and contentment: the presence of God. God had told him and demonstrated again and again that "My grace is sufficient for you, for my power is made perfect in weakness" (2 Cor. 12:9). God's constant presence in the midst of Paul's hardships altered everything. Paul could remember his own sufferings honestly, telling the truth about them, but he remembered them well, without anger or retaliation toward those who had harmed him. Their attacks became an avenue of blessing and strengthening for himself—and for others. He ended his defense of suffering by saying, "That is why, for Christ's sake, I am content in weaknesses, in insults, in hardships, in persecutions, in difficulties. For *when I am weak, then I am strong*" (v. 10, emphasis added).

How strong can we become? At the end of World War II, when the liberators came to Ravensbrück, the Nazi prison camp for women, the same camp where Corrie Ten Boom and her sister were taken, this prayer was found on a scrap of paper in the pocket of an unknown child:

> O Lord, remember not only the men and woman of good will,
> but also those of ill will. But do not remember all of the suffer-
> ing they have inflicted upon us: Instead remember the fruits we
> have borne because of this suffering—our fellowship, our loy-
> alty to one another, our humility, our courage, our generosity,
> the greatness of heart that has grown from this trouble. When
> our persecutors come to be judged by You, let all of these fruits
> that we have borne be their forgiveness. Amen.[13]

I don't know that I could pray this prayer, if I could love my enemies with such purity as this prisoner, who endured unspeakable
evils. But this truth is found again and again: even in the greatest
sufferings, fruits can be borne in the lives of the wounded that can
ripen into healing and goodness for many. All of these—Buechner,
Allison, Ruby, the apostle Paul, the girl at Ravensbrück—were
given the strength not to erase the harm inflicted but to bear the
pains inflicted without infecting others. They became stronger,
wiser, and in this strength, they broke the all-too-human cycle of
hurt people going on to hurt other people.

I wish I could find that seventy-five-year old woman still consumed and broken with anger toward her father, who died decades
ago. I would tell her it is even now not too late to forgive him. It is
not too late to heal her memories. Each time we return to our past,
remembering our fathers, our stepmothers, our fathers-in-law, we
have the opportunity to reclaim the past and tell a truer story,
beyond the deceptions we have all woven about the guilty and
the innocent. We each can tell a truer story that begins with our
human failings—our parents' and our own—and the presence of
God in the midst of it all, shepherding us toward a better love. A

love that finally disarms the haunting, the hurt and trauma, of what others have done to us.

I realize I need to tell truer stories from my own life. If I could, I would take back some conversations that haunt me, one in particular. I remember moments shared with a relative after a death in the family—the bitterness in my voice, the acrid memories I spoke as I spilled my hurt. I saw those caustic words pass into her and infect her, and I see the bitterness playing out in her life even now. It wasn't enough to tell her what happened. I needed to tell a fuller, truer story. I ask God, and her, for forgiveness.

My father is gone now, but his story is not over; neither is mine. I am beginning to tell a larger story to my children about my father. They seldom ask about him, because they did not know him, but they will ask. I am preparing what I will say when they do.

"What was your father like, Mom?"

"He was a loner. He did not have many friends. He loved to read, especially about sailing. He was strong. He was not a bad man. He just had to be alone. He couldn't seem to help that, wanting to be alone. He couldn't make friends or be friends with people. I used to be angry about that, until I saw how sad his own life was, how sad and empty it was to live away from others, to live without loving others."

"Did he care about anything?"

"He cared about words and books. He wanted to be a writer when he was young. I got my love of books from him."

"Did he love you?"

"I never thought he did. But in the last year of his life, I saw ways that

he was trying to love me. He had very little money, but he saved what he could. When he died, we each got a thousand dollars, nearly all he had in the world."

"Did you forgive him for the things he did?"

"Yes, I did."

"Did that take away the sadness?"

"Not the way I thought. In some ways forgiving my father has widened and deepened the sadness. I used to be sad only for myself and my siblings, but then when I came to love my father, I was sad for him. And I was sad for my mother as well, who never had a husband. But I learned a better way to be sad."

"Do you miss him?"

"I do. I miss caring about him. And would you believe I even miss worrying about him? But I have memories now, new memories that make me smile. Remembering now, through forgiveness, has made me well."

AFTERWORD . . . WITH DR. JILL

"Forgive and forget"? No. Forgiveness requires remembrance. A precursor to modern-day psychology is the premise by Greek philosopher Socrates, who said, "The unexamined life is not worth living."

Our memories are important. Memories link us to our lives and keep our existences intact. God allows us to recall some of our memories as needed, and some He keeps recessed for our own protection until we are ready. Dissociation, as discussed earlier, is one form of self-protection in the midst of unbearable situations. Heinous memories can be shut out of awareness, compartmentalized, or locked away. Experiences we have at a preverbal age are registered in the body, or manifested through our senses, leaving us without words to help us understand. Sometimes we just don't have the words yet.

Having our lives make sense is crucial to our sanity. When events are of a traumatic nature, memories may not always flow as easily. Whether they come easily or not, acknowledging who we have been validates the little girls or boys inside of us. We don't need to dig up every detail from our childhoods in order to heal. To reclaim our pasts, we must be willing to look at what we do know, to name it, to have compassion for ourselves in having lived through it, and to grieve our losses. We will process our memories for a time, as they come up, but we do not need to obsess or force them: we let them pass through us. The purpose of remembering is not to hold on but to release and in forgiveness to move forward lighter and freer.

A few weeks ago I received a message from my cousin. My aunt, his mother, had passed away from ALS. My father did not attend the funeral service. When I was young, he had always claimed the importance of family, but he was nowhere to be found. Neither did he show up at his own mother's funeral sixteen years ago when I was pregnant with my first child, or to his father's military burial three years before. He probably was unaware that one of his brothers died last May. Now his sister was gone too. So many lost connections and lost opportunities to heal brokenness.

At the funeral, my cousins, now men, lovingly and honestly choked on their tears while laying their mother to rest. Later, both cousins separately expressed their sorrow about my dad. I thought, *Who? What? Why are they sorry for* me *at their* mother's *memorial?* It struck me later that they were full of their well-lived connection with their mother and were sensitive to the lack of connection I had with my father, their uncle. In some way, whether they realized it or not, they were extending an invitation to me to grieve with them the loss of my parent who had been dead to me for years. They knew I had no body to claim, no ceremony to experience, just my memories to fill the void of an abrupt departure long ago.

As we move forward and claim the life with Christ we are meant to embrace, we will have moments to pause, to remember, to feel a twinge of old familiar pain. This is "normal." After all, healing is not the erasure of hurts, but the erasure of their power to control us. Forgetting is not our goal. Our past is a part of our story, all of it. Moving forward is not pretending that the events of the past did not have an impact. Instead we need to "remember well"; we must relish the character we have developed as a result; and we must use it now to help others.

Leslie and her siblings made an intentional choice conjointly and individually to reach out and help their father. They sought out the opportunity, and they did it on their terms. They were each adults who had taken charge of their own lives and healing. Each had created networks of people that now give them the love and support they lacked from their father. They reached out to their father as an extension of their healing journeys and from the fullness of taking in the sacrifice Christ made for them. They chose to have a new ending to their stories, one in which they had some say. They had hope but not false illusion. They did not need their father for their emotional sustainability. He, in fact, seemed at times unaware and unmoved by their sacrifice. At other moments there were glimpses of his surprise at their generosity and his awareness of his lack of deserving their attention. Certainly in his attempts to cope with his own life, he had more than kept them at bay, seeking safety over relationship and the encapsulated solitude of his own internal world. But their sense of security is in their Father in heaven, who does not shut them out.

This is the hope they wanted to extend to their earthly father. Not all of us have the same tangible opportunities to choose from. However, we each have a choice in how we will live out the rest of our stories. We can choose to reclaim our past for good—instead of replaying the same story over and over expecting something to change in the unending repetition. We do this by allowing ourselves to grieve, to mourn, to lament, to remember, to release, to revive, to live on, so that *all may be well with our souls.*

Study Questions

1. When you hear Joel 2:25—"I will *restore* [repay, make up for, give back to you] the years the locusts have eaten . . ."—does

redemption for what has passed seem possible for you? If yes, then there is hope! If no, then more time is needed in reclaiming yourself from what was lost.

2. You are not your lost past; you are part of the present and can seek God to intervene for your future. Can you make a distinction between what happened to you because of your parents' sin and mistakes and who you are, in spite of them, because of Christ?

3. Forgiveness is an active process. It takes time but doesn't happen with time alone; you must intentionally pursue it. Name some ways you have chosen to pursue forgiveness of your father or mother.

4. Ever feel like complaining to God about all the wrong and hurt you've experienced? Isn't rattling off lists of woes to close friends *for a time* part of processing? Once heard, emotional healing can take place. Does your view of God include this?

5. David knew God could handle his pain as he cried out in anguish in many of the psalms: "I cry out to the Lord; I plead for the Lord's mercy. I pour out my *complaints* before him and *tell him all my troubles*. . . . I am overwhelmed . . . Hear my cry, for I am very low" (Ps. 142:1–3, 6 NLT, emphasis added). Have you allowed yourself a time of telling God all that's not right as part of your grieving?

6. When you look back and think about all the ways you have tried to cope with your hurt, how does embracing truth and new awareness of your parents and your past affect you moving forward?

7. In your journey of forgiving your parents, is there anything you are excusing in them or blaming in yourself that is still holding you back? Are there areas in which you still need to forgive in yourself?

8. Do you ever wonder if God has the same value and belief in you as your wayward parent? If so, what steps can you take to reclaim the truth of God's love for you and His hurting for what happened in your life?
9. Can you write three ways God redeems you? Why?
10. Read Jeremiah 29:11. What is your present understanding of the purpose and plan God has created for your life? What are you doing now, along with God, to self-parent your strengths and purpose?

Becoming Joseph: Into the Land of Freedom

As I walked out the door toward the gate that would lead to my
freedom, I knew if I didn't leave my bitterness and hatred behind, I'd
still be in prison.

—Nelson Mandela[1]

We have toured the land, traveling through the countries of our childhoods, through the deserts of disappointment with our parents. We've seen ourselves lying beside the road, beat up, bleeding. We've seen them there as well. We've looked into our own hearts; we've seen God's forgiving heart and know He offers full forgiveness to all of us—and we know how much we need it. We've entered the rooms of the dying and seen what can happen with mothers and fathers even there. We've looked behind us to see what can be made of the mess of the past. And we're not done yet. We have a few more people to follow who will take us these final steps into the rest of our lives.

We'll follow a man named Joseph, who will take us much farther than Jonah. Like Jonah, he landed in a foreign land, a place he didn't want to go, living a life he never would have chosen. We remember that Jonah went to Nineveh reluctantly to preach a message of forgiveness he didn't believe. Joseph trudged off to Egypt under compulsion as well—his brothers bound him and sold him as a slave, wanting only to be rid of him.

Some of us may feel this way. A parent, a stepparent, a grandparent takes us captive, and we are each dragged off to a place we don't want to go. Our childhoods are stolen. The land we are taken to is oppressive. We want only to escape. Joseph did as well. Yet Joseph did something we are learning to do: he transformed his own slavery and the land of his hardship into a place of freedom and life.

If you know Joseph's story already, you know the serpentine twists that morphed him from favored son to household slave—landing him in the depths of an underground prison—and eventually, through his own faithfulness and God's favor, to the highest authority in all of Egypt, second only to the Pharaoh. Egyptians bowed to him, trumpets blared before his arrivals, and the spoils of the country were his. It was a new day and a new life for Joseph. Let's look at his story now.[2]

———

Joseph stands in his dining hall, his eleven brothers before him, the very ones who had wanted to kill him but who'd settled instead on selling him and making a profit. They have walked the same long trail into Egypt that Joseph walked into slavery, but they are bound by hunger, not ropes. They have come to buy grain from the only country with grain to spare. Because of Joseph. He has saved the nation from a killing, seven-year drought.

They are all together now, in this room, to share a meal, all twelve brothers and what lies between them: ignorance, a history of quarreling among themselves, and a dull wound of guilt that cannot heal. Eleven are crudely dressed, shepherds from dusty, distant fields who know nothing of Egyptian finery. They squirm in their discomfort under the strange gaze of the lord who has called them here.

Even now, in such an unlikely place, they think of him still— how he had begged them for his life, how he was dragged behind the camels like an animal, how they had thrust his robe, shredded and bloody, into their father's shaking hands. And their father's face—it had changed that day, and they hardly remember what he looked like before. They are bound to each other by their guilt, and even now, they lean toward one another, murmuring, accusing, wondering.

Joseph watches his brothers intently. He cannot believe how they have changed. They look old, tired, hungry. They do not know him, of course. How could they? He had never expected this, a chance to confront them, to charge them with all they had taken from him. He'd never forgotten that he was a foreigner in exile from his father, from his beloved baby brother, from his own country.

He listens to their hushed conversations, emotions roiling. Their voices, their mannerisms, their quarrelings—all of it as familiar to him as his own voice and body. Finally, he knows he is about to burst. "Leave us!" he shouts to his stewards who are serving the meal. They glance at him, shocked at his tone and his face. They hurry out the doors.

Joseph steps closer to his brothers and calls them to his side in their own language. "Come close to me."

The brothers go rigid. He spoke their tongue! *What is*

happening? they wonder. *Is this a trick? Has he brought us here to kill us?* They search his face, fearful.

He is . . . crying? The ruler of Egypt is . . . weeping?

Joseph gasps for a breath, then announces—in Hebrew, again—"I am your brother Joseph, the one you sold into Egypt!"

They lock their eyes on his face, terrified. Can it be? If it is Joseph, they know they are going to die.

But the lord is still weeping. He says words they can hardly understand:

"Now, do not be distressed and do not be angry with your-selves for selling me here." He pauses, takes another great gulp of air. "It was to save lives that God sent me ahead of you[,] . . . to save your lives by a great deliverance." He looks at them hungrily, wait-ing for them to respond.

They cannot move. How can this Egyptian be a Canaanite? How can he be their brother?

Joseph steps closer and throws his arms around Benjamin, the brother he was closest to, sobbing. Then he pulls the others around him, and they come, yielding, beginning to believe it is him, their own flesh and blood, the son of their father, their brother, the one they knew they had betrayed. Joseph weeps over them, over each one: for himself, for fifteen years of betrayal, sadness, and exile— and for them.

The family is reunited. Not one is lost. Joseph moves his father and all his brothers' families and belongings from the desolate deserts of Canaan to the land of Egypt, where they are given the best land to settle. All things are new for them. They thrive in their new country.

It's an astounding story. We read these words and we wonder, how was it possible for Joseph to forgive his brothers? What could be worse than one family member plotting the death of another? Can freedom really come out of the depths of such evil intent? I know it is possible. Not just because I believe the words of Joseph's story, but because I know others who have forgiven the unforgivable.

Among her memories, Vonnie recalls a car trip. Her father suddenly pulled off the road to park by a river. Vonnie was six or seven. Without a word of explanation, he took her out of the back-seat and held her in the crook of his arm and carried her into the water. She didn't know what he was doing, but she knew her father was a man to be feared, who could do anything he wanted. He said nothing to her as he waded into the river. When he was knee-deep, he swung her down, grabbing her by her ankles, and submerged her head underwater. She struggled, tried to pull her-self up. He laughed. He'd dunk her under; then pull her up for a few seconds, then dunk her again. She kept fighting to right herself, until suddenly she knew, somehow, that God was with her. And God said to her to be still, to not fight. When she stopped resisting, her father grew bored with his sadistic game, let her down, and on they went, not a word spoken. Vonnie has been afraid of water all her life.

A few years ago, she started going back to church. She was anxious about returning, afraid of being judged, but the church welcomed her and her family.

Months later, Vonnie and two of her sons wanted to be bap-tized. They went out to the lake with the rest of their church. Vonnie stood on the shoreline and told her story to everyone gath-ered there: what her life had been like as a child, all that she and her siblings had endured. About her mother wanting her to shoot her father. About the nightly abuse, the dunking in the river, how her father had taunted her and perhaps had even tried to kill her. "I am so afraid of water," she told them shakily.

When she had finished speaking, her pastor took her arm and walked slowly with her out into the lake. "Are you ready?" he asked gently as they stopped and turned. "I'm going to let you totally dunk yourself. I'm not going to do it. You go down into the water, and then come up out. And know that you do this in the name of the Father and the Son and the Holy Spirit."

Vonnie dropped down to her knees in the water, completely submerged. It felt as if time had stopped. She burst through the surface a moment later, exultant. She knew baptism was a picture of resurrection, of new life, the washing away of her old life, and it was. As she returned to shore, those watching ran out into the water to meet her and hug her. "Welcome to the family!" everyone exclaimed. They were the best words she had ever heard.

Vonnie is no longer afraid of the water. Her father had used water to threaten and torment her; but God, her real father, used water to heal and cover. Vonnie is healing, and she has forgiven her father, though she does not know if he is dead or alive. She has released him from the heavy, innumerable debts he owes her, debts he can never repay. Others see her forgiveness as weakness. Vonnie knows it is strength and courage.

The stories of forgiveness are all around me, people walking from one land to another. Keven looked often to the events in Joseph's life and understood them. His own family abandoned him. Keven spent decades trying to figure out why they didn't love him and take care of him, as parents are supposed to do. He spent decades mourning. But like Joseph, he knew he wasn't in the place of God to judge them. It was God's place to judge; it was his to forgive.

Forgiveness is so powerful, it flourishes even in the most devastated places imaginable. Yes, in Joseph's dining hall in Egypt, in Vonnie's and Keven's homes, and around bonfires in one of the most ravaged countries in the world.

The documentary *Fambul Tok* takes us to a village in Sierra Leone. The villagers have gathered around a bonfire to talk over the day's events, to settle disputes, as is their custom. Sahr, a young man who can barely walk, stands and begins to tell of the horrors that befell his family in the recent war. For eleven years, this *fambul tok*—"family talk," a centerpiece of village life—disappeared in the violence of a civil war that left fifty thousand dead. It was one of the most brutal wars in Africa that routinely conscripted child soldiers, forcing them to kill and mutilate on command. Sahr has kept his own grief silent these many years, but he must speak out now.

He tells about his father's brutal murder, his own vicious beating that left him permanently crippled. Then he goes further: "The man who beat me and killed my father is here." Sahr stumbles over to a man in the shadows and pulls him into the firelight. It is Nyumah.

Nyumah and Sahr had been best friends growing up. But during the war, as children, they were both seized by the rebels and forced to kill. Sahr was given a knife and was told to kill his own father. He refused. Nyumah was then given the knife, and with a gun to his head was told to kill Sahr's father. He did. He also inflicted the injuries that crippled Sahr.

They had not spoken during the war, nor have they spoken since, though eight years have passed. Now Nyumah is called out in front of the community, and he confesses his crimes. "But what I did," he finishes, "it was not my choice." He bows to the ground, and facedown, asks Sahr to forgive him.

Sahr assents, speaking his forgiveness, releasing his old friend from a debt he could never even begin to repay.

Sahr's forgiveness changes Nyumah's identity from murderer to fellow villager to neighbor. The two embrace, as they had as children. All those gathered begin to sing as the two hold on to each other. The unforgiveable has been forgiven.[3]

Though it appears painless in the documentary, none of these mercies were cheap or instant. They weren't for Joseph either. When we look closer into his extraordinary grace toward his brothers, we learn more.

After their father Jacob died, the brothers were fearful again that Joseph would exact vengeance upon them—vengeance they knew they deserved.

Joseph called them together. His brothers came, prostrating themselves, saying, "We are your slaves." They were indeed, and Joseph could do with them just as he liked. But instead he spoke words that surely surprised them. "Don't be afraid. Am I in the place of God?" (Gen. 50:19). He *was* treated as God by the entire nation of Egypt, yet he had not forgotten his true identity: just a man, imperfect. He knew that God was the appointed judge, who alone knows the heart and who alone knows true justice. So before God, Joseph relinquished his legal right to judge and condemn his brothers.

But he was not done. While he would not judge as God, he would still speak the truth about them. He did not attempt to erase his brothers' murderous intent. "You intended to harm me," he began (v. 20).

Nyumah and Sahr, too, had to face and address the brutalities that happened that day in Sierra Leone. They could no longer run from it. Freedom began for them the moment they spoke the truth to one another. Many of us in this book have discovered the same.

But there is no lasting freedom here in this truth-telling alone. Facing the truth of the world as it is and of who people are will free us from deception and self-made fairy tales, but there is little hope for more until another recognition comes. Joseph took that next step, realizing a greater truth: "You meant evil against me; *but God meant it for good, . . . to save many people alive*" (Gen. 50:20 NKJV; emphasis added).

Surely Joseph and Vonnie, Sahr and Nyumeh all wanted those years back, the years their youth was stolen, the years spent in hiding, in slavery, in prison, hungry, in want. But Joseph recognized that his brothers' murderous intent was not the end of the story—rather, just the beginning. He recognized a deeper reality, that family dynamics—indeed, all human events, even those charged with hate and harm—can be swept up within the purposes of God and transformed for the good of others. For Joseph, the outcome of all he lost was the saving of millions of lives, in Egypt and beyond. It meant as well the saving of his own family, who, without the food he had stored in warehouses, would surely have starved. The deeds of the past could not be undone, but they had, mysteriously, through God's hand and through Joseph's own integrity and faith, become the means of his family's rescue—and the rescue of an entire nation and its neighbors.

We do not often see such large-scale deliverance. Most of the time the deliverance is quieter, smaller. I have looked into Vonnie's face, listened to her story. In the documentary, Sahr's face is peaceful. These are people who have found healing and freedom from the hardest things in the hardest places. Yet most of us aren't in their company. Most of us have parents who did *not* mean it for evil, whose lapses and failings and absences were not intended to wound. They would take it back if they could. Many were in the grip of illness and circumstances they did not know how to change. They were weak, without understanding, trying to make their way without resources, not knowing how to raise children. Most did not mean it for evil, but even if some did, God was still present, and He still intends to use it for good in our lives, and for the good of others around us.

Joseph's forgiveness changed everyone's lives, not just his own. He brought his family from a land of bitterness and hopelessness to a land of plenty, where they were given special favor. They never had to worry about food or protection again. The family was restored, whole again, not one missing.

Vonnie has created a warm, loving home and has many friends whom she supports, all far different from the way she grew up. She has reached out to the rest of her family as well.

In Sierra Leone, Nyumah helps Sahr on his farm, and he has built Sahr a new house—with a tin roof, a luxury his friend could never have afforded himself. After work on their farms, they walk together arm in arm, as best friends do in Sierra Leone. The community has begun to heal through their example. And the two are now traveling around the country, telling their story, bringing reconciliation to other villages.

I confess that when I began this book, in the midst of my own last years with my father, I could not have imagined any of this. What could I possibly expect from a man with schizoid personality disorder, who could not form relationships, who was the epitome of detachment and self-entrapment? What could I expect from an old man near the end of his life? How could any scales ever be balanced? How could it possibly turn out well for me? With a houseful of children, a marriage, and a schedule and a life that sucked the marrow out of me every day, how could I afford the risk and exhaustion this would mean? Couldn't I just let him go, that sad, pathetic lump of a man whose only achievement was siring six human beings, one of whom he molested, all of whom he seemed to disavow?

When I first dared to imagine any good at all, I imagined it for myself, to be freed from my own apathy and hate, as so many psychologists, pastors, and radio personalities promised. I heard their promises: I could be freed from my own bad feelings. I could be liberated from obligations to the difficult others in my life.

But as I have listened to others' stories, as I have prayed, studied, and written my way through these pages, my eyes and my heart have widened week by month by year, chapter by chapter. I have come into a much larger freedom than I first imagined.

I had worried that releasing our fathers and mothers from our own blame and justice lets the guilty go free. I did not want to pardon the guilty. But I have been given the means now to step down from the judge's bench and transfer my father from my judgment and sentence to God's utterly just sentencing. Here is freedom: to release ourselves from the roles of prison guard, jury, and judge over those who have hurt us and to hand the gavel and the key back to God, who was always the only rightful possessor.

Standing in this new, vast land, I am learning that forgiveness is about even more than releasing ourselves as judge and jury, and even more than releasing our mothers and fathers from their debts against us. I am learning that forgiveness is strong enough to break generational sins. That it is so powerful it opens our hearts rather than closes them to the sufferings of others. We began this journey to ease our burdens, to set ourselves free, yet along the way we discovered even greater freedoms: the freedom to love the unlovely, to risk hurt and betrayal by others, and to forgive, seventy times seven.

Forgiveness begins with us and changes us first, but genuine forgiveness will not end there. It empowers us to reach out to our families. Through us, it can reverberate out into the wider world, bringing the only lasting balm to the "universal disaster of sinful brokenness."[4] (See chapter 3.) Forgiveness, in its fullest state, leads us to love.

Can we really heal the hurts of the world? How can one person change anything in a world so immense and so badly fractured? We begin by asking the questions Libby Hoffman, the executive producer of *Fambul Tok*, poses to her audiences around the country. After viewing the film, many want to go and help with the reconciliation work in Africa. She urges them to take that desire and go back to their own homes, their own neighborhoods, asking, "Who do I need to forgive? Who do I need to apologize to? How can I help my community be a more whole community?" We start at home, in our own houses and communities, she advises. We start with us. "When we become people who are humble, courageous, forgiving, we're making humility, courage, honesty, and generosity more powerful in the world."[5]

Also, paradoxically, we will find that the more we forgive, the less offense we take from others, the less we need to forgive. We become people of peace, who see their own faults first above others' faults, people who are not easily offended, who need not constantly defend themselves against perceived insults, slights, and threats. As we grow in maturity, we are less and less constrained by protecting ourselves and more given to risk ourselves for the sake of others.

The first steps we take toward our distant fathers, our grand-mothers, our mothers-in-law, our alienated brothers, are steps that lead us toward other relationships, other communities where our own failings and others' have separated and alienated. We go to those places in humility, knowing we have all sinned, that we all stumble in many ways. And we go in strength, because we are not alone. The Holy Spirit empowers us. The church stands behind us. We can find support from prayer groups, pastors, priests, therapists, friends, neighbors, and other family members who will walk forward with us. If a group like this doesn't exist now, create one. We don't have to be lone rangers. We have made forgiveness too private, too small, and too hard. It is not a feeling we have to conjure up; it is an attitude of humility and love that seeks the good of the other, apart from worth or deserving. It is the living out of a daily decision to extend to others what God has extended first to us.

And now, what has come of my forgiveness of my father? My life is full of other people who stumble in many ways, just like me. There is no end to my own need for forgiveness from others, nor of the need to extend it to others.

While beginning this book, my husband and I agonized over leaving a church where we had been members for many years. After five years of wrestling and struggling, we left. I harbor losses and disappointments from our years there, not only for me but for my children. My fingers touch those wounds continually . . . and here it is—another realm where forgiveness must be sought and pursued.

At one of my sons' after-school activities a man I didn't know who was new to town e-mailed me to tell me that one of my sons is unruly and everyone is afraid of him: something must be done. I sucked in my breath; my stomach shrank. This is the son who listens to everyone's problems, who cries with those who are sad, who walks around wanting to fix everything that's broken. I wanted to fire back an angry e-mail, but I checked myself, and instead, I talked with the other coaches, then later with the man himself. Together we discovered a different problem. By God's grace, that problem was resolved. I could forgive and let the mistake go. The man and I are now friends.

My six children, now ages eleven to twenty-five, will need to forgive me, imperfect parent that I have been and will continue to be.

In my marriage of thirty-six years, there are events and whole years I would like to forget. Instead, I am working to reclaim the past, through the lens of forgiveness. My husband is choosing to forgive as well. And if we are to continue together for thirty-six more years, we will need to daily pray, and to daily walk out, "Forgive us our sins, as we have forgiven those who sin against us" (Matt. 6:12 NLT).

I am just beginning. I am just learning to live a forgiving life, putting on the habit of mercy, choosing not to take offense, choosing to remember the depth of my own offenses, choosing to find joy in blessing rather than cursing others. So many people are ahead of me: Keven, Dena, Jeanne, Laurie. What will our freedom look like in this new country? It may look like inviting our fathers, our mothers, our in-laws, those who have sinned against us, to our dinner tables and our homes. It may even look like sitting at someone's feet.

A few years ago I sat at my mother-in-law's feet, just a few weeks before her death, cutting her toenails. I had never seen what eighty-six years of life does to toenails; neither had I ever sat at Wanda's feet before. She was a woman who loved to work and serve others; who taught school, piano; who helped run a ranch, a fish camp; who raised three boys. We shared so much of our lives, but we were very different from one another. But that day, to sit at her feet and serve her this way was poignant and freeing.

Jeanne's rocky relationship with her father was eventually healed through forgiveness, but she was alienated from her husband's entire family in another country. Jeanne and her husband took a month-long trip to that country, hoping, praying to reconcile with all of her in-laws. Cultural differences had come between them, and Jeanne herself confesses that she was ungracious, self-protective, even "a jerk" at times.

She apologized to each one, saying, "I'm really sorry for offending you. You're my sister in Christ. We're going to be connected for eternity, so let's enjoy it now." The whole family responded, and doors and tables and phone lines are all open now. "The most devastated ruins can bring forth beauty if you are open to it," Jeanne tells me. She and her husband and two children, all musicians, now tour the States with a message of reconciliation.

Dena was trapped in bitterness and anger and saw God as an angry, vengeful father much like her own father. Forgiving her dad took away her anger and opened her eyes to who God really was. Dena told me, "As I began to get free, I naturally wanted to share that freedom with others, and God has opened multiple avenues of ministry—writing, speaking, online relationships—where He has used my past and the healing He gave to encourage others."

Laura has come a long way toward her father. Restoring that

relationship, forgiving and being forgiven, allowed her to simply love him as he is, flaws and all. But even more, she tells me, this freedom to love and be loved "as is" transferred to other relationships. It enabled her to lay down sharp resentments with coworkers, and even more, it has improved her relationships with men in general. "Most of all," Laura wrote, "it's allowed me simply to delight in Dad, and in others, instead of wanting to change them . . . and to bask in the delight that is reflected back at me."

After her father's suicide, Sheryl decided that her marriage and her family would be different: her house would have open doors and no secrets. Her own four children have brought through her doors gangs of friends whom she has befriended and nurtured. Her past will never disappear, but the force of the present fills her days with purpose and joy.

Keven was able to release his parents, especially his mother, and break free from hurt and self-pity. "I stopped feeling sorry for myself," he told me. "That burden of trying to figure out why they didn't love me and take care of me was gone. It didn't matter anymore, because God replaced all that with other people who cared. He freed me up to care about the people who didn't care about me."

Vonnie's forgiveness of her parents changed her profoundly. "Forgiveness grew me closer to God and made me want so much more. It gave me a real hunger to love the people around me."

For all the power and good that comes from forgiveness, know that we will not do it perfectly, not any of us. We will be beset by our own limits continually. But the imperfection of our forgiveness does not negate or limit its value, its beauty, and its rightness. Every act of forgiveness, Miroslav Volf has written, however incomplete and provisional, however tenuous and tentative, however based on our own faulty judgments of others' faults, it still is an echo of God's own forgiveness. And the day is coming, he wrote, when the brightness of God will illuminate all the black corners of our hearts and lives. We will know God's love so fully and truly, we will know and experience His own forgiveness so completely, that "we'll make God's forgiveness of the sins of those who have offended us fully our own. Our forgiveness, now tarnished, will then sparkle in its full splendor. We forgive now in hope for that day."[6]

———————

I return to the day we were all gathered in my father's room at his nursing home. Five siblings and my brother Clark's three teenage children were there. The room was tiny, with just a bed, a dresser, a chair, and a TV. We were a mob, perching wherever we could find a space. We were all turned toward my father, who sat just a few feet away from us on the edge of his bed. He was wearing a beige shirt with green stripes, the khaki shorts Laurie and I had bought him. He was shaved and alert.

I blinked with wonder. It had been sixteen years since we'd been together. Now our family was reconstituted around the very one who split us apart so many years ago. We had come, each of us, to bless him however we could. Our tongues faltered; we stuttered, speaking the language of blessing, a speech we did not hear growing up. We knew he could not live much longer. We offered what we had—our attention, our presence, hoping it was enough. My brother Scott, who has borne many burdens from my father, more than most of us, showed him photos of birds he had taken while in Florida. Clark drove three hours each way to visit him on the weekends. Yesterday we drove him back to the marina where he lived on his little sailboat for thirteen years and took him out for ice cream. We were doing all we could think to do.

But one of us was missing. Our sister Jan could not get off work to fly down and join us. We wanted her to be there with us in those minutes. Laurie decided to call her on her cell phone. She dialed, then waited for the ring and the answer, all of us watching her. Jan picked up, and Laurie's eyes lit up.

"Hi Jan. This is Laurie," she said. "We're all here in the room with Dad. Do you want to talk to him?" She smiled into the phone, looking around at us. Laurie handed the phone to him. He took it hesitantly.

We watched our father talk to a daughter he had seen once in twenty years, the same story as the rest of us. She had flown down six months ago to see him. I didn't know it at the time, but Jan had reached out to him two years earlier and had called him as often as she could. She had forgiven him his failings before me and had wanted to bless him with her calls, her concern, her attention. The conversation was unhurried, like the others, but this one different. He could hear, but he processed slowly after the stroke.

"Hi, Jan," he said in his bland, unmodulated voice that neither asserted nor denied.

We heard her voice but not her words.

"I'm doing okay." Pause.

"Good to hear your voice." He did not look at us as he spoke, but we were all eyes on him. I had never seen my father speak on a cell phone to one of his children.

I remembered Laurie's and my visit a year ago, when we had shown him photos of each of our families and where we lived. He didn't ask about our children or our lives, but we wanted him to know who we were, who we had become. All the days we were there, he never asked about his other four children.

I looked around the room at my siblings and I thought of Joseph in the dining hall with all his brothers, the reconstitution of his own family, how unlikely—how impossible, even—it was. No one but God could have made that happen. The ten older brothers sitting below him had ended the life Joseph had known some sixteen years before. But their intent to harm had not utterly destroyed Joseph's life; neither would he let it destroy their own lives. He knew he had a part to own: he had been obnoxious and foolish, feeding his brothers' resentment. But he had repented of his own pride. Joseph knew well before that day that he would offer them forgiveness, blessing rather than curses.

Our father had wounded every one of us in significant ways, but we had all decided the same as Joseph: We would not pay back what was given to us. We would forgive. We were there to bless.

I heard Jan talking, trying to keep the conversation going, but she was struggling, as all of us did, even before he got old. She was ending the call. I heard her say, "I love you, Dad."

"I love you, Jan," my father answered back. A blade pierced my side; tears stung. I looked around the room, with wide eyes. Did everyone else hear it? Had he ever said *love* before? And he called her by name! I knew these were just words, spoken even perhaps just reflexively, but he spoke the very words we were living before him that day. I never heard him say *love* again.

I had learned to give with extended, open hands, expecting nothing. Yet I carried a sheaf of new memories now: this word today, the afternoon we wept together, the sentence he wrote in my notebook, a glance over lunch, a "happy birthday" he spoke on my last birthday. It wasn't everything I wanted from my father, but I had decided it would be enough.

Joseph entered Egypt as a slave—yet there he found freedom and offered it to those who least deserved it. In that tiny room with my father, I felt a great joy that God had freed me to love the man in my life who least deserved it.

I have found what others have found before me. Choosing to forgive does not relieve all burdens. It does not free us from attachment and obligation. Instead, it brings a burden, but it is a worthy burden. And we will not know how light this yoke of love and forgiveness, how fitting the habit of mercy, until we step into it, wrapping it around our shoulders. We will feel then the full force of forgiveness, its power to lift and strengthen and move us from a land of bondage out into a full, spacious country with open gates, our hands open to all.

AFTERWORD . . . WITH DR. JILL

Ahh . . . there is life after hurt, where the air is fresher, and our hearts are lighter, where we can laugh, and sing, and dance again—not as if no pain had ever existed, but with the knowledge that we have grown in character. We are wiser, and we have a new purpose.

Sure, we can identify with Joseph. Many of us were taken to places we didn't want to go and forced into situations we wish we hadn't faced. Thank goodness our hope lies beyond our circumstances, and that what our parents may have intended for evil, God can use for good, just as He did for Joseph. And Joseph forgave.

Joseph's forgiveness process was not immediate. During his years in jail he had plenty of time to imagine how it would be if he were ever to see his brothers again. He'd lived through the horror of being disowned, betrayed, and rejected by those closest to him, the very ones he was meant to trust, his own flesh and blood. I imagine he experienced the same emotions the rest of us have, including those whose stories we've read in these pages. Imagine Joseph's feelings of shock, abandonment, protest, justified resentment, aloneness, sadness, hopelessness, gut-wrenching despair, resignation. No doubt, there were countless replays of his childhood betrayal. Perhaps he bargained with God, and certainly he cried out to Him at his darkest moments. Then finally, surrender— to the only One who could save him. And God met him in his dark place.

When the opportunity finally came to see his brothers, though filled with emotion, Joseph did not react impulsively. He kept a safe distance, maintaining appropriate boundaries, and tested his brothers over months of time to ascertain the level of risk he might face, before opening up to them again. Had they had a change of heart? Could they be *trusted*?

Our questions should be the same. We can't assume, just because we are ready to forgive, that those who hurt us are ready to engage in reconciliation. We do not need the offender's remorse or repentance in order to *forgive*, of course. However, without that repentant response, we cannot be *reconciled*. Sometimes we receive degrees of conciliation, where both sides overtly or covertly agree to disagree—a sort of truce—to move forward. True reconciliation, however, requires the offender's humbled response to his or her wrongdoing. Can he *identify* with you in your heartache? Can she see *your* perspective regarding the hurts she caused? Have they developed *empathy* for your suffering?

For an offender to respond in these ways, however, also requires something of us: that we tell the truth. Joseph acknowledged the truth. He did not pretend the betrayal never happened. "You *intended* to harm me," he said. He let his brothers know, in no uncertain terms, that what happened *still* happened, and it was wrong. But then he moved from blaming his offenders and wanting them to pay, to looking at how God paid: ". . . but God intended it for good" (Gen. 50:20; emphasis added).

Even that knowledge, though—that God can bring good out of evil—can leave us hesitant. Often, because of the wounds inflicted by those who have hurt us, we refuse to allow *anyone else* in. To move forward, we must take risks with people who haven't hurt us; we must allow God and others in before we can confront our deepest wounds.

If, because of your deep wounds, you have not allowed anyone else in, it is important to start somewhere by taking small risks. Trust is built through repeated exposure to minor risks that increase as people prove trustworthy. We develop the ability to respond in relationally sensitive ways to minor or unintentional infractions that realign their trustworthiness but allow for human imperfection.

———

Regardless of our offenders' willingness to enter a process of healing, we must move forward, with or without them. Following God's call to forgiveness is something we do, because we know it is right and good for us—and right and good for the world beyond us.

Study Questions

1. Do you ever feel like Joseph? His experience and story teach us a lot about life after heartache and tragedy and about the power of forgiveness. What parts of Joseph's life journey do you identify with?
2. Reconsider Genesis 50:20 in light of your family circumstances. Are you able to gain some perspective on how God's greater good trumps man's evil intents in your life?
3. Compare Jonah's versus Joseph's attitudes and reactions. What are the differences you note between them? When and in what ways have you been like Jonah or like Joseph in your attitudes and reactions?
4. What qualities of character were cultivated in Joseph through his difficulties, during his years of separation and estrangement

from his family? How did God's timing serve him and prepare him to extend forgiveness to those who had done harm to him?

5. Do you ever imagine a healing reunion with your family members, as Joseph had with his? What if your family, especially your father or mother, do not see their part? Are you also able to consider extending forgiveness even if your outcome differs from Joseph's? What might that look like for you?

6. Describe the difference between forgiveness and reconciliation. What would have to take place for you to have both in your specific situation? Which comes first?

7. While Joseph forgave his brothers, he did not trust them immediately. What can you learn from Joseph about re-establishing trust in ruptured relationships? What graduated risks are you willing to take in regaining your ability to trust others after what was broken with your parents?

8. Each narrative chapter of this book demonstrates aspects of the forgiveness process. Following each of the chapter summary phrases, try to express how you connect with each progressive phase and where you see yourself in the forgiveness process.

    · *Running, avoiding, or hiding from what's true. What's your story? What tugs on you that you need to do?*

    · *Confessing; naming hurtful truth and generational sin to another.*

    · *Humanizing your offender; seeing your shortcomings; developing a sense of compassion.*

    · *Allowing time to be in touch with your hurt, anger, protest of wrongs; assessing when bitterness, resentment, and unforgiveness have taken root.*

    · *A matter of your heart. As God forgives you, can you also choose to forgive?*

- *Honor people, not dishonorable acts; choosing to honor by being honorable.*
- *Forgiving through loss and grief; developing mercy; being a part of God's legacy.*
- *Remembering well to release your bondage and reclaim your past.*
- *Extending forgiveness; being open to reconciliation; establishing healthy boundaries; learning to trust; because of Christ, choosing a higher calling for yourself, others, and the kingdom of God.*

9. Specifically name where you are making progress from your list above and where more work needs to take place. Share your success with a trusted friend and ask him or her to support you as you journey on.

10. What is a next right step for *you* in *your* forgiveness journey?

ACKNOWLEDGMENTS

LESLIE LEYLAND FIELDS

Though I live on two faraway islands and have every claim to solitude and independence, I cannot begin or complete a manuscript without the help of others.

My agent, Greg Johnson, has been a tireless and always available supporter of this book. You are a treasure, Greg, always generous with your knowledge and assistance.

Meaghan Porter has been a superb shepherd of this project, with the perfect editing ear and eye.

The Thomas Nelson art department created a stunning cover in record time. (I was so impressed!)

The wonderful staff and people of Emmanuel Faith Church in Escondido invited me, by faith, to speak from a book that wasn't quite finished. My enriching time with you confirmed again God's choice and timing of this book.

Finally, I want to acknowledge the many who were willing to share their hardest stories with me. Some here I have known for decades; just as many are new friends who took a chance in speaking to me. I could not have illuminated the hurt, risk, and freedom of forgiveness without you.

May all of us believe and practice it "seventy times seven."

—L.L.F.

Dr. Jill Hubbard

To all who have found forgiveness a difficult mountain to climb, but in hearing the calling, were willing to risk the journey. Pushing upward through each painful, even treacherous, ledge to find peaks of freedom, hope, and a better way, one rocky step at a time. Your attempts are glimpses of a higher call and are honorable reflections of being children of the Most High. This book is for you at whatever point you find yourself on God's path.

Thanks to Greg Johnson of Word Serve Literary Group, who foresaw a fit in our writing duo by inviting me to accompany this vision. Our editing team deserves thanks as they meticulously read every word to hone our message. And all at Thomas Nelson who help turn manuscripts into books, get them into the hands of readers so lives can be touched, thanks for what you do.

I'm humbly grateful to those who've personally walked with me through my own struggles of forgiveness. And especially thankful to those who revisited forgiveness topics during this project as I wrestled with not putting words on pages but conveying a message that's real.

Lastly, and most importantly, I want to thank Leslie Leyland Fields, for being willing to share her intimate story, her beautiful expressive writing, and allowing me to add input alongside her. Thanks for walking this project through numerous obstacles—its message was worth it.

—J.H.

Notes

Introduction

1. Irene Mecchi et al., *The Lion King,* directed by Roger Allers and Rob Minkoff (Burbank, CA: Buena Vista Pictures, 1994), DVD.

2. Harriet Brown, "How to Forgive Others—Health Benefits of Forgiveness—Fred Luskin," April 27, 2011, http://www .oprah.com/oprahs-lifeclass/How-to-Forgive-Others -Health-Benefits-of-Forgiveness-Fred-Luskin/print/1.

3. Caroline May, "The Number of Babies Born out of Wedlock in the US Is Soaring," *Business Insider,* February 21, 2012, http://articles.businessinsider.com/2012-02-21/home /31081751_1_illegitimacy-black-children-unmarried-women.

4. Childhelp, National Child Abuse Statistics: Child Abuse in America, http://www.childhelp.org/pages/statistics.

5. Rodney Clapp, "The Sense in Which Love Is a Felony," audio clip, http://imagejournal.org/page/news/rodney -clapp-reading.

CHAPTER 1: BECOMING JONAH: RUNNING FROM OUR STORIES

1. Irene Mecchiet al., *The Lion King*, directed by Roger Allers and Rob Minkoff (Burbank, CA: Buena Vista Pictures, 1944), DVD.

2. Bible verses in the Jonah story are from Jonah 1.

3. Patricia Hampl, *I Could Tell You Stories* (W. W. Norton), available at http://www.nytimes.com/books/first/h /hampl-stories.html.

4. John 8:32.

5. Dan Allender and Don Hudson, "Forgetting to Remember: How We Run From Our Stories," *Mars Hill Review* 8, 65.

CHAPTER 2: DARING TO CONFESS: THE SINS OF THE FATHERS

1. C. S. Lewis, *Till We Have Faces* (Orlando: Harcourt, 1984), 249.

2. L. Gregory Jones, *Embodying Forgiveness: A Theological Analysis* (Grand Rapids: Wm. B. Eerdmans, 1995), 299.

CHAPTER 3: BECOMING HUMAN: THE DEBT WE SHARE

1. Quoted in Susan Emerson, "Awakening our hearts to others' pain," *GloucesterTimes.com* (Gloucester, MA), April 8, 2011, http://www.gloucestertimes.com/lifestyle/x1075332536 /Awakening-our-hearts-to-others-pain/print.

2. Aleksandr Solzhenitsyn, *The Gulag Archipelago: 1918–1956: An Experiment in Literary Investigation*, vol. 1 (Boulder, CO: Westview Press, 1998), 168.

3. Eugene H. Peterson, *Tell It Slant: A Conversation on the Language of Jesus in His Stories and Prayers* (Grand Rapids: Wm. B. Eerdmans, 2008), 185.

4. Fyodor Dostoevsky, *The Brothers Karamazov*, chap. 41 (pt. 2, bk. 6), at the Literature Network, http://www.online -literature.com/dostoevsky/brothers_karamazov/41/.

5. L. Gregory Jones, *Embodying Forgiveness: A Theological Analysis* (Grand Rapids: Wm. B. Eerdmans, 1995), 126.

6. Peterson, *Tell It Slant*, 185.

7. Jones, *Embodying Forgiveness*, 126

8. Peterson, *Tell It Slant*, 185.

9. "The Good Enough Mother," Changing Minds.org, http:// changingminds.org/disciplines/psychoanalysis /concepts/good-enough_mother.htm.

CHAPTER 4: THE UNFORGIVEN
AND THE UNFORGIVING

1. Mahatma Ghandi, *Young India*, April 2, 1931, repr. in *Collective Works of Mahatma Ghandi Online*, vol. 51., http:// www.gandhiserve.org/cwmg/VOL051.pdf.

2. This is part of the book's subtitle.

3. Amazon.com, author Christine Gallagher's page, http:// www.amazon.com/Christine-Gallagher/e/B001KHSBEE /ref=ntt_dp_epwbk_0, accessed January 11, 2013.

4. Promotional description of *The Woman's Book of Revenge*, RevengeLady.com, http://www.revengelady.com /bookofrevenge.html.

5. Miroslav Volf, *Free of Charge: Giving and Forgiving in a World Stripped of Grace* (Grand Rapids: Zondervan, 2005), 160–61.

6. David Webb Peoples, *Unforgiven*, directed by Clint Eastwood (Los Angeles, CA: Warner Brothers, 1992), DVD.

7. David A. Stoop, *Forgiving the Unforgivable* (Ventura, CA: Regal, 2005), 16.

CHAPTER 5: THE HEART OF FORGIVENESS

1. C. S. Lewis, "On Forgiveness," *The Weight of Glory* (1949; repr. New York: HarperCollins, 2001), 182.

2. Dylan Thomas, *The Poems of Dylan Thomas*, Daniel Jones, ed., rev. ed. (New York: New Directions, 2003), 162.

3. The following story is adapted from Luke 15:11–32.

4. Eugene H. Peterson, *Tell It Slant: A Conversation on the Language of Jesus in His Stories and Prayers* (Grand Rapids: Wm. B. Eerdmans, 2008), 185.

5. Peter Filardi, *Flatliners*, directed by Joel Schumacher (Los Angeles, CA: Columbia Pictures, 1990), DVD.

6. *As We Forgive*, produced, edited, and directed by Laura Waters Hinson (Los Angeles, CA: Mpower Pictures, 2008), DVD.

CHAPTER 6: THE PRODIGAL FATHER AND
MOTHER: HONORING THE DISHONORABLE

1. Paul Weitz and Nick Flynn, *Being Flynn*, directed by Paul
Weitz (Universal City, CA: Focus Features, 2012), DVD.

2. Albert Camus, "Return to Tipasa," in Philip Thody, ed.,
Lyrical and Critical Essays, Ellen Conroy Kennedy, trans.
(New York: Knopf, 1968), 165.

3. J. I. Packer "Why Holiness is Necessary," *Living Bulwark* 58,
March 2012, http://www.swordofthespirit.net/bulwark
/march2011p3.htm.

CHAPTER 7: LORD, HAVE MERCY:
IN THE LAST HOURS

1. Czeslaw Milosz, *Selected Poems: 1931–2004* (New York:
Harper, 2006), 162. Excerpt of three lines from "The
Separate Notebooks: A Mirrored Gallery" from *The
Collected Poems 1931–1987* by Czeslaw Milosz. Copyright
© 1988 by Czeslaw Milosz Royalties, Inc. Reprinted by
permissions of HarperCollins Publishers.

2. "Ed's Story Ask Forgiveness Clip 02," YouTube video, 0:57,
posted by "edsstory," July 18, 2012, http://www.youtube
.com/watch?v=DhTSYKbZ_Gs.

3. Chris Provenzano et al., *Get Low*, directed by Aaron
Schneider (New York: Sony Pictures Classics, 2009), DVD.

4. L. Gregory Jones, *Embodying Forgiveness: A Theological
Analysis* (Grand Rapids: Wm. B. Eerdmans, 1995), 126.

5. C. S. Lewis, *The Four Loves* (New York: Harcourt Brace, 1960).

6. Miroslav Volf, *Free of Charge: Giving and Forgiving in a World Stripped of Grace* (Grand Rapids: Zondervan, 2005), 220.

CHAPTER 8: AFTER LAMENT: RECLAIMING THE PAST

1. Tom Robbins, *Still Life with Woodpecker: A Sort of Love Story* (New York: Bantam, 1980), 277.

2. Lewis B. Smedes, *The Art of Forgiving: When You Need to Forgive and Don't Know How* (New York: Ballantine, 1996), 171.

3. Patricia Hampl, *I Could Tell You Stories* (W. W. Norton), available at http://www.nytimes.com/books/first/h/hampl-stories.html.

4. L. Gregory Jones, "Healing the Wounds of Memory," in L. Gregory Jones and Célestin Musekura, *Forgiving as We've Been Forgiven: Community Practices for Making Peace* (Downers Grove, IL: InterVarsity, 2010).

5. Frederick Buechner, *Wishful Thinking: A Theological ABC* (New York: Harper, 1973).

6. Frederick Buechner, *Telling Secrets* (New York: HarperCollins, 1991), 33.

7. From the United States Declaration of Independence, 1776.

8. Larry Crabb, *Shattered Dreams: God's Unexpected Path to Joy* (Colorado Springs: Waterbrook, 2001), 31.

9. Timothy Keller, *The Reason for God: Belief in an Age of Skepticism* (New York: Penguin, 2008), 182.

10. Ibid.

11. Crabb, *Shattered Dreams*, 4.

12. Allison Backous, "Blessing the Past," *Image*, February 17, 2011, http://imagejournal.org/page/blog/blessing-the -past?comment=9823.

13. Quoted in Erwin W. Lutzer, *When You've Been Wronged: Moving From Bitterness to Forgiveness* (Chicago: Moody, 2007), 131.

CHAPTER 9: BECOMING JOSEPH: INTO THE LAND OF FREEDOM

1. Quoted in Hilary Rodham Clinton, *Living History* (New York: Simon & Schuster, 2003), 236.

2. The story of Joseph's revelation of himself to his brothers is found in Genesis 45. Dialogue is taken from the NIV.

3. Fambol Tok (film), produced and directed by Sara Terry, 2011. For more information, see http://www.fambultok .com/about/synopsis.

4. L. Gregory Jones, *Embodying Forgiveness: A Theological Analysis* (Grand Rapids: Wm. B. Eerdmans, 1995), 126.

5. Quoted in Tim Heiland, "A More Sustainable Peace," *Prism* magazine, July/August 2012, 37.

6. Miroslav Volf, *Free of Charge: Giving and Forgiving in a World Stripped of Grace* (Grand Rapids: Zondervan, 2005), 220.

ABOUT THE AUTHORS

 LESLIE LEYLAND FIELDS is an award-winning author of eight books, a contributing editor for *Christianity Today,* a national speaker, a popular radio guest, and a sometimes commercial fisherwoman, working with her husband and six children in commercial fishing on Kodiak Island, Alaska, where she has lived for thirty-six years.

 DR. JILL HUBBARD is a clinical psychologist and regular cohost on Christian radio's nationally syndicated *New Life Live* program. Dr. Jill has gained a reputation for her gentle and insightful style of connecting with radio callers. She lends a woman's perspective to addressing callers' psychological and spiritual concerns. She is also in private practice where she sees clients who struggle with depression, addictions, eating disorders, and relational and personal growth issues. Dr. Jill lives with her family in Southern California.